War Memoirs

18th July 1939 – 27th January 1946

E. R Gamble

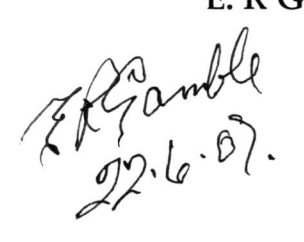

Published 2007 by arima publishing

www.arimapublishing.com

ISBN 978-1-84549-181-9

© E R Gamble 2007

Newspaper Extracts © The Weekly News D.C.Thomson&Co.,Ltd

All rights reserved

This book is copyright. Subject to statutory exception and to provisions of relevant collective licensing agreements, no part of this publication may be reproduced, stored in a retrieval system, or transmitted in any form or by any means, without the prior written permission of the author.

Printed and bound in the United Kingdom

Typeset in Palatino Linotype 13/16

This book is sold subject to the conditions that it shall not, by way of trade or otherwise, be lent, re-sold, hired out, or otherwise circulated without the publisher's prior consent in any form of binding or cover other than that which it is published and without a similar condition including this condition being imposed on the subsequent purchaser.

swirl is an imprint of arima Publishing

arima publishing
ASK House, Northgate Avenue
Bury St Edmunds, Suffolk IP32 6BB
t: (+44) 01284 700321

www.arimapublishing.com

I spent 5 years on apprentice with a branch of Vickers namely Robert Boby Ltd, of Bury St Edmunds. When I finished in July 1939 my last shift was a 12 hour night shift on war work; that was a good job done. I thought I was entitled to a holiday before somebody else got other ideas, so I joined the malisho for six months as a 21 year old.

Cambridge was the place selected for the medical test by seven doctors, my result was A1. My father wasn't at all pleased when he heard. I heard of three more lads being called up. They gave the offer of what I wanted to go in, I wanted the tank corps, that was full, next choice R.A.O.C, but when I received my destination it was a field of tents which was chiefly flooded of Oswestry in Shropshire. We four should have gone on Sunday, I rang Cambridge who said go Monday. Lorries met the trains and convoyed us to the camp.

Monday morning - sort out when lorries arrived loaded with sleepers to lay down in the mud. Young officers fresh from Sandhurst, thought they were going to get them laid before we had our tea, but we shouted 'we want tea' and the sleepers went everywhere, the mud also flew and caught the officers who soon called it off!

Tuesday - we had a parade to draw wellies where we had to wash. Shave meant standing in about six inches of water, our toilets were open air with a pole across a trench.

Up at 7am parade at 8am with clean wellies. After parade, blankets folded up neatly and placed outside on the duck boards covered by our ground sheet, 8.45 we stood by our kit while the B.S.M and orderly officer would inspect each one, and glare at your chin to see if I had shaved, if not name taken for fatigues.

Later Tuesday - we went to draw P.T. kit shorts, plimsolls, vest and shirt, then next it was uniform. Mine - 1st World War jacket which went round nearly twice, Bedford cord breeches and puttees, 2 pairs of boots. Then come the breaking in of boots and cords by having to crawl on the ground no matter what came in the way and pushing through hedgerows etc.

Marching on the road was for our boots to soften up. We were in the Kings Shropshire Light Infantry 140 to the minute start 2 miles and working to 15 with full pack of 70lbs. Before leaving the B.S.M. would come behind to feel the weight, anyone getting heat blisters report to the M.O.

When on route marching anyone who had dentures was given haversack rations of a round of bread, those who had their own teeth were given two large biscuits 4"x¾. It took a hard blow on the knife butt to break, our dog loved them.

After a week we were given a walking out dress of grey flannel trousers, navy jacket and black beret. Our first trip out was to see what Llangoller was like as a small town.

Two girls came forward and wanted to show us where a farmer had to shoot his son who was with a girl he didn't approve of last week. When we asked what time the last bus went to Oswestry they said 7pm only to learn later it was 5pm, so it was a case of foot it just 12 miles. We got caught going into camp other than the correct way.

There was a light restriction guard on he accosted one lad who hit him and tied him up with his gas mask strap, another one came in my tent after me as I had left a small light showing, so I spent the rest of the night in the guard tent under arrest.

Monday morning - 8am after parade I fell in with escort. The Sergeant Major came along behind me and knocked my tin hat off in the mud, so I stepped out and picked it up and put it on again, so again he knocked it off, and growled "Leave it there, it will be there when you come out, if you do!"

The Captain read out my charge of endangering the lives of 5000 men, so the officer asked what this man is like at drills, said he can't say "I have not seen this man before." He was quite right as I had not handed my card in which said 115 BTY searchlight malisha depot, he awarded me 3 fatigues. (1) to peel 15 carts of potatoes by hand, (2) help to lift a piano on to a lorry (as I was only 5'1" I could walk under it), (3) to move 12 ¼" tent boards on to a 3 wheel trolley and pull through mud 5" deep. So it was prisoner and escort right turn quick march. I picked up my tin hat when he dismissed me, and went to my right lot up the other end of the field, they didn't get many spuds peeled cause I didn't go down there much. If there wasn't anyone in the cookhouse when we finished our lot sometimes I borrowed a large tin of fruit and condensed milk to share in the tent, we did quite well really.

Nobody told us or showed us how to keep the puttees with tape from falling down, a corporal amongst several returned from India, he showed me the trick to get over that, mark them L & R. They gave no more trouble of being picked up by the M.P.s for being improperly dressed and given 7 days confined to camp.

While at Oswestry they couldn't give us marching drill because there was only mud, we had instead trained on the search-lights. I was a sound locater other lads were spotters, engineer for generator, and cook, they worked as a team out in the wilds somewhere.

To give us a change of scenery they took 3 coach loads of us down to Swansea to guard the docks, we went on a large ship for food etc. I had a month there and went on pairs. One night the duty officer came round in an Austin 7 on challenge he didn't stop so my partner stepped forward to push his bayonet through his radiator. The officer got out and just said he didn't hear or see the sentry, so we pushed his car to the side and left it.

The day our coaches returned September 3rd as the towns were all out and the territorials in Leominster were on parade and told us war had started. Back at Oswestry the R.E.s (Royal Engineers) had taken the search-lights over they had all gone. So they took on the firing range for us, we went by lorry somewhere to have a proper test, we had the 303 Lee-Enfield rifle. I must say I had a good one; it got me an extra three shillings a week for getting 4 bulls out of 5 at 1000 yards. The infantry officers said that was good and if you do that again I will see you get a better rifle, I didn't go anymore.

Our time now is coming to a close at this Oswestry dump, drafts were put up on notice boards containing the names of men and where they were going. I was lucky, I was posted to Connaught Barracks, Dover 5th Field Trg Regt. Some went to Dover Castle to learn signalling. There another split into different squads under regular Sgts. An officer came on morning parade and said step out anyone who has a civilian driving licence. I wasted no time he was a regular M.T officer in charge of the garage where gun tractors were kept. On Wednesday drivers reported to the garage and were given jobs getting to know the gun tractors, we had a real marching drill in between, on the board I saw gym so I went sick from parade to see the M.O and get excused of P.T & gym. I told a white one he looked at my scar, which was a years old acute appendix op, so he gave me a card that I report to the garage, wonderful!!

They had no battle dress for us yet, so it was still breeches and puttees, polished toe caps, confined to barracks until satisfied for guard mounting was strict guard Sgt followed by B.S.M, duty officer next, he would pick out the best man to be attending man, his job to wait on the guard. I got slick-man twice, a thankless job. On a 24hr back flight, the food was good there cooked by H.T.s and plenty of it.

I was taken on a driving lesson by my namesake, his initials were R.E.G the reverse of mine, he said he lived in Bury and worked for Johnsons in St John Street who were butchers. I had to take an army driving test having passed that with good results and duly made up to a driver mechanic that meant as extra 6p a day big money?! Being in Dover with the bombing and air raid it was where the lads came in to go on leave from the B.E.F and return from shaft barracks. After the war, a medal was struck called Hellfire Corner.

I left Dover for Southborough our billet an old jam factory we had to march to the drill hall each morning a mile to Tunbridge-Wells, where my days were spent on old cars and lorries the gunners had old 18 pounders. I remembered 30 from Dover to make up the strength of the Maidstone Sat Nighters to become 386 BTY 143 Field Regt. We used to go out on schemes around Tunbridge and places in those old vehicles. I was given an old Austin 16, the clutch was about clapped out, so on most hills I had to reverse up, the lads had to get out and walk up.

One morning I reported sick with a sore throat, I was taken to East Grinstead Hospital, two weeks in there and I was told I was better as they said I could return to my unit. I was put on the bus for Tunbridge so very handy I caught the train that was waiting ready for London and went to Liverpool Street station, I got to Bury St Edmunds, I felt proper poorly so went to my doctor. I had a high temperature and went home to Risby and bed, he visited me. About 3 days later a buff envelope arrived with a very kind letter saying 'return to unit in 48hrs or steps would be taken to affect my misapprehension'. They received the doctor's letter, which made a mountain of difference by return of post, I received ration cards for 2 weeks and a travel warrant to say 'travel when fit'. Signed W. H. Hamilton Laugh. March 19th we were moved by train to Tetbury to train and march to Weston-Birt in tents once more.

What vehicles we had were in a field by the coach and horses our officers billet. We drivers after B.S parade were going to be taken on a test of driving by the new major Hamilton. He got to know each man's name in the BTY. So in the car, being the best one available, he took one at a time in order of name for his driving test, no comments. We went down to Okehampton to fire and calibrate the new 25 pounders. While we were out on the range new vehicles had arrived, staff cars and lorries. The MT Sgt had a list and called out the names of each man to stand in front of the vehicle as he called the named driver. Low and behold I was the first one to drive the C.O. this being a Hamber Snipe 27HP. In that day arriving back at Westonbirt collected a pass for 7 days embarkation leave, this faded out, so went to a place in Dorset called Powerstock the guns guarded the coast here we slept in the tracks placed under trees etc. except when the lorry was called for a job, then all ones kit was removed and covered under the hedgerow with your ground sheet until its return. I left my great coat in the 3 tonner when the detail was to take some lads to Bridgeport, the sods only cut the sleeves of it, a lesson was learnt. We used to go to Yeovil for a bath at the helicopter factory, think it was Westland then.

We had a roll call at 6.30 am for a run, we would go fast while in the sight of the Bdr (2Stripes) then drop into tall bracken by the roadside. I and some more would wait till all had passed then double back to our wagon's lines. This wasn't a very good position. On one scheme I was to drive the C.R.A Top brass as Ham called it, flag on the bonnet fluttering in the wind it was, his vehicle a Vauxhall when I heard from the rear the noise got louder and the prop fell off the coupling to the differential with a clatter to end his ride, as I stood by the roadside I saw the 144 Field Regt pass, and a lad called out to me he used to work at Boby's before joining up.

While I was at Powerstock the farmer needed help on his farm some of the drivers went to help him. I had a cockney lad who had never seen a horse hoe, where one person leads a horse in the middle of a row of small plants while pulling a 2 wheeled hoe. These then adjusted to cut the unwanted weeds from the centre of the rows. This cockney lad took the hoe right along the row cut out the plants and left the weeds, he thought the garlic was pretty, maybe the old farmer wasn't pleased with our hoeing.

Another day it was hay turning after being cut and dried, it was our task to put it in haycocks, which was to stand it up into heaps about six feet high and the same base, it was very hot for the work and the farmer went and brought back a gallon cask of rough cider, 'have a drink boys' he said, about ½ hour later all one could see was eight pitch forks standing by the haycocks the boys were all asleep, so much for cider.

Blandford Hall drive, it was a terrible place about 3" of dust under the trees in tents. I will remember this joint for two reasons. One, we were going out early so we went to cook house for bread and marmalade as it was dark I didn't see the rear end of a wasp, but I soon felt his tail, I was soon in trouble as my tongue was swelling quick, I ran down to the M.O and to Blandford Hospital, he said what I had done, two tablets given in the mouth and 5 minutes all was well. So was able to drive my old friend Ham (C.O) out.

On return Charlie Sarby came running to the car and saluted Ham eventually he got out what the trouble was. Bdr Sheering had sunk Toc (carrier) in the river which runs through Blandford, we washed the vehicles down on the bank but Ginger wanted to know how far it would jump. The river was 8 foot wide he would have been ok if the opposite side was flat but the carrier slid back into the water and sank, the seats floated away and Ginger had to swim back, Ham gave him 48 hours to get it running or he would be on a charge he lost one stripe. The carrier after several months rejoined us in Alatoss Iceland. He was using a tin to scoop out the mud, I went to see how he was getting on with the job, when I pressed the starter it gave a suck and blow. The engine was full.

Hursley Park Winchester. We had been to inspect this area when Ginger was having fun previous day. This was a good place being near to the town if the old buses were full at night they had a ladder at the rear we would wait until the driver was in then and scramble for the ladder, for the roof on a bend it would veer over, so the tyre rubbed in the mudguard. Ginger was instigator of this. We could see the fire on Southampton docks from this camp the place kept us guessing, there were medical checks and some lads went off. Then we saw different kit arriving and heavy twill like coats, other boxes had the words. Alabaster stencilled on them, queer to us, got a map to see where this pace could be. Without success. Fresh signs were painted on the vehicles a polar bear, 49 DIY core sign that was it, I believe it was early September 1940, I had warning to fill up the petrol etc, a long drive ahead so we left Hursley early hours our column stretched 15 miles, I was doing just 12mph all the run to Glasgow. Ham (CO) standing up and watching the distance between the trucks we would stop to watch them go by us, he could see the guns were having a job to keep up doing 55mph, so they had to come up front doing a steady 14mph he would tell me I was doing 1mph too fast. We had a night car camp. All up check round, and kip down and off next morning about 10 am heading for Scotland, steady old 12mph in top gear going for Dunkeld according to his route card making our final to Glasgow we took just 3 vehicles to Gerock for loading on the deck of a destroyer, waited in for Lord Gort who came on our advance party, one day out one of convoy with our extra kit got hit said goodbye. There was an AA gun fitted to our boat they fired it as one didn't answer signals it blew the top structure away, I was down low under, the piano food was brought up by my pals, Old Lord Gort had a parade each morning but he didn't see me. I went from the first night and saw my first day light at Reykjavik as marine's pulled us up by our rifles, no proper unloading after a stormy rough trip doing a zig zag 3" each way for 3 days and nights it was nice. Put my feet on dry land again an oil company had their sign just the reverse to the Gerry Swastika, we thought several things it was Iceland. I think it was the middle of September. We had a wonderful night on concrete floor a blanket and great coat as one would say a great night. The Lord Gort slept well in a heated Nissen hut we saw no more of him. They had rounded up the 100 Gerries who had made a good stretch on concrete road, all of their roads were made of lava on rock. We went to a Nissen hut camp at Alafoss 7 miles from Reykjavik. He had a factory in this making blankets, as the hot river was there, boiling water coming up from the ground. I didn't fancy sleeping on the floor so my pal Stanley went in search of wood, tricky business this, taking a 15 cwt for the job, ventured along a track a farmer fence had got the boards we wanted so Stan went to reconnoitre while I went to turn round for a quick departure. The boards were just tied up having got six the old farmer was coming after us, too late we got our bed boards, four others wanted to know where. Camp entrance wanted making up a bit so truck drivers RS CWT took off to the R.E camp near Reki 8 miles to get filled up, I was waiting outside Ham's hut with the car ready to go out, when Sgt Major my friend came and said take that and get a load of lava no questions, away I went and removed seats and shovelled it in amid some laugh from R.E in the meantime poor old Ham was searching for his car, when I rolled up he was there, where have you been said he, Sgt Major sent me for a load of lava sir. Where is he stamping of hands behind his back brought him back but not in my ear hearing, so I had the job of getting it out, I knew he would get his own back.

Most of our food all came out from England two men were detailed to report to the D.I.D store to pull the leaves of cabbages until they came to best leaves, I had anti scorbit tablets to make up, bread also was shipped out until they built a bakery in Reki.

A troupe camp which was further away from Headquarters got fed up with lamb every day, so they decided to have a change a nice little pig was borrowed from a farm and duly killed and parts hidden until wanted. I drove Ham for Saturday inspection on their camps when he got the message nothing was found, it gets dark in winter at 1400 and light next morning about 10 am.

One had to remove, petrol pump glass, fire extinguishers, distributor cap, and BTY only to rake carry them out in the morning from your hut replace and start the engine warm up run for ½ hour, take your time and it would be ready to take them off again.

Entertainment we didn't get much only what we made, so one day there were three ponies on ground adjoining our camp. So Jim Wilkens, Eric Wells and myself thought of catching them for a ride round the camp, but we didn't get far the old boy lame and dragged us off one by one and made us wait by his small house, he went in and brought out his Mrs to keep us there. She sat on rocks opposite to us, it caused a laugh to see her red flannel draws, down to her knees. But our laugh. He went down to get an officer to come back with him, we were gone over the lower part of the mountain behind his house, laid in scrub he had no sight of the 3 cowboys and we walked on the other side back to camp.

Most of our time was spent training mountain warfare, when enough snow had fallen we would go on a scheme to be taken into the mountains armed with kit, knife trench spade, depth pole, ski's, large black pack and 2 man tent, my pal Stanley who was a heavy sleeper. I had the meths stove going to get a cuppa and the porridge oats ready, with a few grunts from the B.S.M outside. Get up man, Stan turned over and so did the cooker, the tent caught fire, Stan got out sharpish. That was one thing less for us to carry up a rugged mountain, using the long pole to test where to put our feet, we walked until the snow was about 2' deep we then to make a snow house the ski's were placed across the top when up to that height. Me being 5'3" we gave it another inch or two for Stanley, our bed one each end raised two feet off ground it tool us about 2 hours good going. They said we could shoot anything to cook and eat never saw a sparrow, so it was hard luck, surprised how warm it was and a good peaceful night was had by all, so we knocked our hut down and got packed up and ready to descend to level ground, ready for the next lot to do the same, we then had to push the lorries out. That was Pingvellir. One day we had been out all day and it was very cold biting wind in the evening Ham (CO) came in the hut with a rum ration one tablespoon was your lot, this always took the use from my legs, Stan never drank his so I used to bottle it. I had a rest on my bed, the Sergeant came in and said you are guard as one had gone sick, he very kindly said you can be attending man come round when your ready, later I got ready when my legs felt fit, put my ordinary coat on and the heavy one turn up the collar and I was like a staggering tent, duly arrived at the guard room staggered in caught hold of the stove pipe swung round it and fell down in the corner. Rum had drained down to my feet, later when I recovered one job was to fetch the guards dixie of tea from the cookhouse which was over a rocky track, on my way back I caught a rock against the dixie and so they only had about half of it, anything else they wanted the Sergeant let them go themselves attending man wasn't very steady on his feet.

In 1941 we had a visit from the great prime minister Winston Churchill, he stayed quite a few days inspecting the troops, here and having a walk along the concrete road by the Germans before we troops arrived there in September 1940, when the marines rounded up about a hundred Germans they were making blankets at a factory in Álafoss, where they had all the hot water they wanted from the hot bore hole which also supplies boiling water to all houses in Reykjavik by means of an insulated pipe tunnel by the road side.

We also had the celebration on the Kings birthday as a great number of the 5,000 troops came to parade along the concrete road and also parade route a field and the salute taken by the gunner regiment the 143 Field. Maybe Americans have built a road further round this island. They did have a Naafi in Reykjavik in the town itself they had one hotel Borg on the way to the ski club mostly for the officers, so they could have their booze. We got weak tea.

The winter months we had it very cold but it was a very dry cold. But we got strong gales when they blew, it was a job to stand against it, one sturdy gale over 100 mph it sunk four cataleena flying boats in the bay, I thought only one was recovered and lived in by the navy.

In one place near Selfoss near the side of the road mauve and yellow sulphur burns by day and night not a very pleasant smell. Some farmers have cattle and build small churches on the land to avoid them paying tax on their property. Their main animals are sheep black long wool some white, I bought several skins and sent home. We ate lamb every day for 2 years, most of our needs came from England. Sometimes when out walking or on a scheme you might get a square slab on the ground with perhaps a 1" hole in it, leave it alone as on occasions a jet of hot water could rise to several feet, most of the houses in the 40s had imported galvanised roofs. They didn't like the British troops there, first part of our time 4 men and rifle to go out, no associating with the girls, if caught it's trouble.

One night at our Álafoss camp the lads saw a pony nosing in a refuse bin it was eating bread which was thrown in by the cooks so Frankie Woodcock brought it two more loaves and the pony came into the hut, that caused some laughter but the biggest laugh was when they tried to walk it out, one lad each side of it pushing his sides in when a large volume of hot air escaped followed by you know what, glad I was sleeping up far end.

Our vehicles were very poor for the roads round Reykjavik district, Fords had no shock absorbers, on the 3 tonners and Bedfords were not much better a matter of 5 – 10 mph. Some of the lads whose name came at the end of the leave rotor usually were taken further away to the ski club for a week, a terrible journey on the road at very slow speed. I never got there only to fetch them back, but it was nearly a days run there and back. Often the bolts sheered off that held the steering box to the chassis member. My luck was out on one trip just at the bottom of Selfoss pass with four sharp bends did the track rod break, so it had to be first aid roadside treatment, one lad went to ring the BTY, while I got to work with jack knife and a piece of wood from a fence cutting a hole to fit over the bolt and wired it on tight and the same to the other end. The 20 lads preferred to walk up the pass some had piece of rock in case it was a bit dodgy. The BTY sent out a Bedford it was dark when we met, but effort made it and wood remained in my toolbox.

One day Stanley was detailed to collect an officer from Reykjavik dock, he waited for a boat bringing him in, but on the dock side he saw two boxes nobody claimed them while he waited, so he popped them into his truck, back to camp one had 24 tins of Canadian bully, that was smashing so he split it, well worth borrowing. I found the last one in a locker before handing the car in, the other box had 24 tins of nestle condensed milk we enjoyed that.

We had to travel to a small river a semi rotary pump had been fixed up with a pipe leading over a petrol burner to the spay head. So the particular day I operated the pump which was about 6' from the spray, when they all had their bath and got back into the lorry there was no one left to operate it for me. Big joke a 2 tape (BDR) said you're on a charge for refusing to have a bath. I didn't answer him. So in the morning after 930 parade I duly went up in front of Ham (CO), he read out the charge, have you anything to say? Yes, sir as I pointed out the layout to him and said my neck didn't stretch that far, so he choked the BDR off, and said if you bring another man before me like this I will demote you, case dismissed. Right turn quick march out.

The roads were not very good only lava dust and foundation, to travel, near the edge, the peat will give and if you are unlucky to go over or in a ditch or river as I found out was a stream in my case.

A ½ shaft broke one being used from another Humber, was not very satisfactory being tested by the fitter once it slid across the road and down the bank, on its side. There was no damage to the car for its venture, but we could see the cause when laying on its side a split pin missing from the linkage, mum was the word.

On one scheme out all day, it came to the time for something to eat that required water joke, Sgt Major said empty water bottles into a dixie, they didn't get enough so those who had no water and empty bottles would go without, no need to say I was one of them, that was more weight to carry but back at camp the old so and so put us on 60 arms bend, but was raining on our return that had a mission our kit for here was good. We had white hats with peak ear flaps and tapes for the chin. We had oiled socks 2 pairs, boots 3 sizes to big, hob nails in the soles, no polish just water-resistant dubbin, (Fine) our overcoat had 4 linings.

With the collar up I was covered, we only did 1 hour on and 2 off during the winter months, it gets very low temperature we had neat glyco (special anti-freeze) in vehicle radiators. The ice got very thick on the small lake where the Icelanders used to saw ice lumps about 2 feet thick then load them on an old lorry also on the ice taken to a place and crushed for their cod.

That procedure was great the cod was gutted and tied in pairs and hung over wire lines by the roadside could be 30 yards long and had 3 or 4 lines behind each other. The vehicles made a cloud of dust covered the cod grey, the rains came and washed the dust off, still they hung there, for a week wet and dry before being collected on an old model T Fords with tip up lever. On one occasion I was walking down the street in Reyki a truck tipped up and they lost the lot, and others just ran over it, that did stink. In our days just one street round the town, no made up pavements there.

The summer it never gets dark, one could write at 1 or 2 am and see northern lights moving across the sky, a wonderful sight.

The soldiers billeted in the Reykjavik area all had to supply men and lorries round the clock to transport the lava rock etc for the making of the Keflavik airport, the R.E's (Royal Engineers) broke up the mountains and loaded the lorries, the R.E's blasted the mountains to obtain length and material for foundations, when lorries brought it men shovelled it off, they were towed off by crawlers tractors.

The base had more than 12 inches of reinforced concrete and steel, but while it was being leveller an American fighter plane dived low and straight into the blade of a digger that all he knew about it.

The American Marines took over from us, very smart dark green uniform with red piping down the leg of their trouser.

Their vehicles green with red line round it, but we had to leave our Nissen huts for them and go into a large tent the guy ropes being held down by 4' steel bars, during the gale got up and the tent pegs gave up so we had to get up and knock the bars in fresh places. It was a good job they couldn't hear what they were called.

A German fighter plane came to see us one Sunday morning I think it was in 1942 it flew over machine gunning the Tyne Side Scots Regiment, who were on a church parade, several were killed. The Icelandic air force consisted of one small seaplane which took off and landed on a lake, and a skill trainer which flew over our camp to land on the table mountain, so much for them, no ack ack guns out there just them, after that a Boforfor came out.

On Sundays I used to get the job of collecting the padre from Reykjavik Hospital where they lived in ½ a Nissen hut. They gave me a list of camps he wanted to visit for a 1 hour service, he would manage five camps during the day.

On one Sunday I collected the parson from my next village at home Little Saxham he was a nice man and said he could easily get me out if I wanted to, I told him I was happy in the army as I joined to get a holiday and see a bit more of the world, which I did. Sadly Brynley Jones got meningitis out there he was flown home but he died.

There was talk going about that we were packing up here and going back to England.

On April 19th we started to pack things up and get ready for loading by handling in our heavy coats and thick boots. Get ready for the old bull once more back on English soil.

The 25th April was the day a large liner sat at the dock side in Reykjavik waiting to take the whole 49th Division Core Sigh Polar Bear back home, we came back on the Empress of Australia, arrived in Gerock on April 27th. 507 BTY went off first on to train 386 we got off about 1500 hours and train for Ponty-Pridd in South Wales fresh part to see. We were billeted in a disguised church, as we had no vehicles yet our time was spent in the gardens chatting to the girls etc. we had to be inside by 10pm, Sgt Majors orders we had to pass his billet along the pavement but after 10pm boots off socks didn't make any noise.

We didn't stay here long once the trucks arrived at Cardiff. There were several dents to be knocked out after being bumped around in transit. We had 10 days leave from May 4th up at 0400 hours caught the London rattler and got home about 5 pm 14 days leave, went back two days early to London and stayed at Stans in Hampstead. The weather was fine and warm just right for going on the schemes, might have been better if our cooks had a course on how to get tough old beef tender, many weeks on end beef, cabbage, spuds gravy liked coloured water, one slice of bread and jam for tea, good job we had a naafi.

This was a nice little town I don't think we will be here much longer, we're not earning our keep. Ham (CO) has gone on leave and will be amongst us again soon. 2nd in command Basher Bailey is not popular at all now he has a pip and crown up.

Penybont Radnor. We left Ponty 15.6.42 and it was a grand day for a steady run 90 miles in 6 hours arriving about 8.30 to draw palliasse and straw, some contrast from sleeping bags, the tents had been put up ready for us, on a meadow, haven't a chance to explore the area yet, the third day they caught five of us to peel 4 cwt of spuds. One lad Ganny was late back from leave and was on a charge so was awarded fourteen days confined to camp and given hobs to do. Surprising how comfortable one can get on bag of straw if you put enough in. they must have got a stock of old bullock as the beef is just about chewable.

On the 25th June we went out on a scheme to Llandrindad, Bwilth, Llaniloes, Llandilo, Comarthar St Clears, I was driving the umpire, no speed limit today, he was the top brass for 49 DIV. We had a lot of days out, several lads were on charges for one thing or another, late back off leave chiefly and being late in camp at night. One session Stanley my pal found his way to Llandrindad for A.T.S dancing, but one did I don't know how he picked up the wrong hat on that night came Sunday parade that Cap badge wasn't like ours. On charge improperly dressed he was awarded 7 days confined to camp, but he had to get his right hat and badge, that was where I came in, taking the Bren carrier to fill up at the pump not far from the ATS billet so I could swap hats.

On another occasion I went for a walk round the area to discover a plantation of cob nuts, wonderful, having a sample first then went back with my empty gas mask bag to nearly full with husks on, back at our tent and proceeded to remove the husks pushing them between the floor boards in the tent, all was well until Saturday morning when the C.O thought he would look in the tents, bad luck for me, the husks had gone brown at the 1st glance he thought a squirrel had been there, I being nearest to the flap, he said you take those ¼ boards up Gamble and sweep that muck out, how he did guess, he guessed right!

I got caught for a few arms bend for missing 2 pm parade, the old Sgt Major was mostly on my tail, I got over him one night when Stanley Mac and I was on guard we had the 12 – 2 shift to walk round the vehicles the hedgehogs were about. The first one I saw was picked up and put in the car, a 2nd one was captured also and made safe for later. We came on at 0400 to 0600 hours, I took the hedgies across to the old B.S.M tent and lifted the wall and put them inside, hoping he would place his foot on them. I heard of it but a few feelers were put out, he inspected the guard list and hours.

Pete Black and I went to another nutting expedition before they all went and we nearly got caught. We went on PT parade in trousers so lot of us were on cookhouse for five days, but chiefly and being late in camp at night. When we left the cookhouse we weren't empty handed usually, it was tin fruit that was the favourite.

On 22nd November we had some old codger up for dinner it was a job to know what it was meant to be, but burma road followed we had plenty of that, our stay will soon be ending here in time to move on.

22.6.42. Llangorotie after breakfast of dark liver and spuds up at 6 am and ready to move off at 8 am, by the way Builth Wells and Danny Brabin (LT) was soon rounding up sheep for jobs, had a usual of cabbage, spuds meat of some sort, this was a large park, many more soldiers were here some Indians some who roasted an ox every so often. They were out of bounds for us to visit.

Some looked a bit vicious with turbans and big knives. It wasn't long before Captain Mount started the bull s*** up, PT was getting away at 7.30. The canal was at the top of the field one tough Sgt Howard had a brain wave of two ropes across the canal tied of course for us nits to cross for PT hope we would drop in. we had a lot of rats at our last place so Danny Brabin (Capt) thought he would hold signalling classes with morse lamp, that didn't go down very well, when rude messages were being passed.

When the Reme was being formed I put in for a transfer to follow my job as a Horizontal borer, as Major Hamilton was now back and we were out he brought it up and said no to my transfer. I waited for three weeks and put in again, this time he asked if I wasn't happy in the Regt I said yes I was, but he said while he was in command he would not pass it the old ***! On a very nice warm day the 21st October 1942, I wrote to the war office and explained I would like to get a transfer to the new Regt Reme but on the 28th October 1942, I saw Capt Mount making a straight line for our tent, he simply said the C.O. wants you Gamble, going across the park he said you wrote to the W.O. so he has an answer, no anger Mount.

I approached his office with caution when after my knock came a large growl, come in you silly young bugger have you never had K.R.R read to you or parts of it? No Sir! I joined as a militia it wasn't until September 9th when they took my pay book in and changed my number and added to the end of hostilities, the letter had travelled through many departments having got different colour stamps twelve in all, my recommended transfer was one hundred and fifty six days (156) in Woolwich Detention Centre. The good work I had done for him I would not hear anymore. I had put a large blob on my sheet that would stay, all ended up fine and I was able to return to our tent much to the surprise of the other five.

I drove him out in the morning down to Abergaveny not a word was mentioned about it, he knew each man by name. Sunday morning church parade, after a poor breakfast of bacon and fried bread we marched to the Llangotoch village church which was quite nearly a mile, through the park, but on the way back were some chestnut trees that were loaded, we went in noon and sorted some out for roasting after rotten bread on cheese and a spot of jam after.

A session round the fire it was to write a few letters and early to bed. This camp has got is share of little brown fluffy things called mice, so we put some water in an empty bucket and provided them with a run ladder the first catch was twelve, went down to Abergavenny for the evening to see what the town was like and the people, the picture was good, met a young lady called Violet. Went to pictures till 10.30, to walk back for liberty truck a 3 ton truck.

Tuesday 19.11.42 woke up with a sore throat, got up had a wash and shave waited for sick parade at 9 am. Dr Grod had a look at my throat and said go back and keep warm, later 2 AT's came and carted me off by ambulance to Bulch Army Nissen Hut hospital. I wondered if the gear wheels had any teeth left on them they were shocking drivers.

I went straight into bed and soon air lifted to isolation, soon the M.O.E nurse appeared screen round the bed, and a swab taken my throat was followed by a large injection in the arm and had to lay flat for 24 hours. My food, ovaltine and jelly no exercise. Had plenty of company at night, rats ran around, the nurses stayed in their office at night, I had diphtheria now I was on the mend after eleven days I had sausage and gravy for dinner its turkey fried spuds, swede and burma road.

On the 27th November back in the ward, woke at 6 am to mighty great rat eating cake on the next lads locker. Stanley Mac came to see me and stayed to tea. Danny Brabin (Capt) also paid me a visit but I was asleep. Tom Greenaway came in with a large boil on his stomach had to lay up on his back, I had pay parade on the bed, and some mail come in, had a letter from mother 22nd December 9.30 still here in hospital getting a good share of rest and watching the old rats picking up the crumbs sat around until blondie the nurse came on duty, then Tom came with sprained ankle from R.H.Q he had been on assault course. We had a bit of chicken, fried spuds, cabbage. I had to have treacle tart and milk. Had a letter Edith and into bed at 9 pm.

24.12.1942. Somehow I think my stay here has come to an end, a 15 cwt truck has come into the yard, and will take two bod's back to the unit, my pal Stanley Mac was on charge for leaving a truck unattended 7 day C.B most of the evening Mac was spud bashing back to the usual tea, bread, jam and cheese. For breakfast a change to sausage and fried bread, went on parade and followed with P.T went on a bit of semifore class taken by Danny Brabin some dinner came up beef, cabbage and some of Macs spuds burma road (Rice).

8.12.1942. A real day full of jobs started the day, breakfast 7.30, one piece of bacon and fried bread, had p.t. I missed that by giving the hut a sweep through followed by a parade for our nodding Danny Brabin. Then went to his class for lamp reading knocked for Mac but he didn't have many return to his class. Dinner up, stew, spuds, cabbage, burma road not much to jump about on for p.t. at 2.50 a blanco session more bull s***. Inspection my blanco got watered down, next session parade for the hut got washed cleaned up ready to go out after a mouldy old tea of bread and jam went to Abergaveny met Violet and I went to the pictures saw young Mr Pitt out at 9 pm took a walk until 10.30 pm. Then back to camp had a parcel from Macs mother this day and others are from diaries kept at the time. We certainly had some peculiar food it a wonder I'm still here to tell the tale. One lad did get discharged with ulcers in the stomach.

13.12.1942. Not a very good day all considered up at 6 am breakfast at 7 am got ready for church parade at Llangolic a good march left at 9.30 weather normal, rain great coats as it poured down on the righteous, diner as usual was tough old bull and cabbage, fried spuds and duff, could be anything. The afternoon being free got ready 3.45 to go to Abergaveny by bus from Llarrfayem had me tea at the Y.M we went for a walk, came on to train left Violet about 10 pm, caught the truck back to camp, Stanley got in about 10.50 from Llandrindad Wells.

16.12.1942. Woke up 6 am to find it still raining fast so instead of parade we went to Map reading in the hut no escape with Danny he needed some as he generally got lost, that day a change in food, stewed carrots, cabbage and bread pudding, no currants or nutmeg it was still pouring at 4pm so no p.t. I love that!!

Our tea was as good as dinner bread and margarine how could I jump about on p.t. I hardly had the energy to go down to Abergaveny to see my friend Violet, the rain stopped for us it was a walk up a mountain road she knew of back at 10 it was a good night and biked back energy restored.

18.12.1942. Not much to report to this date only they must have found another field of cabbage I had tooth ache come, it helped to get off Danny's class but didn't stop us going up to Crickhowell met two more lads Aherty and tried to dip them in the fountain, went to the phone box to ring home but couldn't get through, wrote several cards and sent them.

20.12.1942. Sunday walk to Crickhowell to get a paper with Stanley Mac returning about 12.30 to have a lovely Sunday lunch more of that old bullock, spuds, cabbage and prunes and custard. Had a rest for 2 hours then a walk to Hanquin to catch the next one to Abergaveny went to the Y.M for tea. It was dry for a change waited at the GPO (General Post Office) until 6pm when Violet came along this evening went for a walk was on the cards to Gilwern took a lane which should have led back but a dead end, that needed extra walking but before completing our

Sunday walk it came on rain as usual, found some shelter until 10pm, saw the lass home, I was really soaked girls!

Owing to the fact that I was late getting in the nice chap on guard put the name in the book so on Monday 21.12. I was given 20 arms bend. This day we had a muster parade when my old C.O Hamilton said cheerio to us lot, we were going to be split up to form another Regt and he was going to take over another lot. I would miss him having been his driver for 2 ½ years, and the many scrapes he got me clear.

24.12.1942. Big day for breakfast a wonderful set up ham and spuds, the saying goes the army marches on its stomach changed our ways about it, bed down and tea a half back to normal bread and jam and cake a show was put on in the NAAFI but no truck was laid on, nobody turned out, Stanley Mac went out to sample the ale. Pete and I went to get trucks ready to go to senny – bridge for gun practice that lasted 2 days. This on the evening back at Penclawdd we met a man in the village who invited us as his guest to the workermens club, the man said his name was Dai Thomas he had a son Melvyn, we were later asked to his home, where many pleasant hours were spent in the company of Mrs Thomas and Melvyn who was about 9 years old. I corresponded through the war years with Dai and then Melvyn after his father died, Mel did well at school. In his time did national service in the Education

Corp which put him in good position to take up teaching when he finished his 2 yrs national service we had a lot of work to do at this camp sometimes I was detailed to go to Newport for new wireless batteries from the ordinance depot.

Back to camp the vehicle park was and required a lot of work on it we had to get rocks to fill up the holes. Dinner at 12.30 still able to find some tough old beef and a change to have some sprouts over cooked. In the afternoon Pete and I were sent up to get more trucks, that's about all they could give us to pass time. The vehicles was a long way from our huts, concrete paths were painted with lime we used 5 cwt, when a big noise came, coal was painted for this, benefit we stood on parade waiting in the hot sunshine 3 lads passed out. The parade section was on grass where p.t. was performed also arms bend with full pack, I must say I did several sessions there anything up to forty. Sunday was a church parade you and your best battle dress, when that was over we would be marched back to camp change to denims and get the car park to work until some of the people wrote to the new C.O who was a right old (B) he was soon given the name of handle bars because the length of his tashe was over 2" long each side. Stanley Mac was over in H.Q. I was glad to stay in a troop. When our car park was ok an old valentine tank was brought for training and unfortunately it had a bad start, the ground had a slope towards an old pond almost covered in weeds and rubbish returning after dinner to see just the turret out of the bushes sorry!! It had sunk.

I was very often out on detail to Newport, Cardiff and teaching some of the new bod's driving. An officer often would set a route he would cruise round on a motor bike to keep an eye on us, damage that was done to property would be repaired and paid for by the culprit.

There was quite a hill at the side of camp that used for p.t. if the N.C.O could hold enough together until he raked the others out, of the huts, after leaving the other camp at Llangotin. Pete Black had his wife lodging at the village of Crickhowell. I had a friend at Abergaveny she was a dentist receptionist. Dai arranged cycles for us, to get to Swansea to catch the early workman's train 0600, Pete used to get on the bus to Crickhowell. I had a nice breakfast at a restaurant, then I waited at dentist house until she finished. We borrowed half a book of passes stamped. Signed we wrote across the top with concession rate, that got a bit off normal fare. I think the ticket man was beginning to rumble us, same two each week. We would arrive back at Swansea approximately 12pm then get our bikes back to Penclawdd about 7 miles, leave the bikes at the house, and nip along the railway line through the wires and into the hut. Most

Fridays I would get a telegram sometime for the next, I put in for a pass then go, my blankets would be folded up as if I was present good mates, sometimes we would go to the pictures. I still have her photo I think back to the days I must have been a nutter.

27.9.1943. We left Penclawdd in the early hours making way for Scotland and mountain warfare training. We had a new CO not a very nice one after Ham, I think we were three days travelling, Motherwell a nice town. The B.S.M was little Scotchman and a bumptious little man.

The lads soon made friends and nearly all had homes to visit, we AP's (Armour Persons) delivered self propelled 105mm guns 28 ton as driver mechanics we had to go on a course to learn about them and maintenance they used 5 gallons per mile. I thought they were just the job, we drove around the slag heaps. We had RME teaching us, I was first to leave the slag heaps for the road, it was easy to lift the kerb flags with the tracks, each one lifted cost the driver 9/- in that day.

One nice trip to collect another one, I was allowed to drive it back from Dankell.

We had a garage to do jobs for the trucks in, the garage owned by Mr Brogan his bungalow joined the garage a window faced the bench a large family, the boys used to come in, John was about 18 years old and helped his dad driving, also a young girl employed in the kitchen, she used to bring a jug of tea in, sometimes I used to go in baby sitting, nice people. Cathie was the lass who worked in the kitchen and often took the micky out of BSM when she came to work, and we were of 9am parade.

Our cooks were a poor old lot on their jobs some of which was uneatable not far from our factory billet, there was a British Restaurant about 100 yards up the street, so about 20 of us one day were enjoying a plate of soup when to our horror the BSM and orderly officer walked in, some slid on the floor, so we had to fall in outside and they found out how badly the food was cooked. They said we would be banned from going in there and eating civilian food,

Washing and shaving in cold water in Scotland winter time didn't go down very well, but it wasn't long before we discovered a big boiler in another part of the mill and the man gave us plenty of hot water, that sucked that little Scottish BSM in.

One Sunday Flash Millson was asked out to tea and take a friend so he asked me, the lady had a daughter in the wrens. We sat talking by a nice fire when I realised I was on guard, I ran all the way back full length of the main street, borrowing mates clean web that was polished up and his rifle, my tin hat, I belted off up the street a bus pulled up I hopped on, I arrived just as the guard had mounted. They asked why I was late so I told the Sgt I was out on a detail. Our guard hut being an old air raid shelter and two hurricane lanterns the place being full of fumes, good to finish this one.

While we were on the invasion exercises off denoon an early morning scramble was called at 0400am to start the S.P's and drive along the beach to an area which had been flooded to 4" deep, we had to drive through the tracks with fire crackers going of all the time.

One drove over them. They thought this was good for the nerves (perhaps). The muddy water was by now bubbling just beneath our visor, another inch it would have come in this window on our laps, and no lights.

On another day we loaded the S.P's on to tank landing barges and over the water to the Isle of Bute. Here tried to climb up a foot high bank into a wood that was a job have succeeded nobody said trees had been cut down and stumps were covered with brambles and rubbish. The day was spent freeing the tracks it started to rain and we got soaked, we got the guns back in the dark and wet. The navy were not there to pick us up so a good fire was lit, they had forgotten us. (typical)

Back to Dunoon and we had Nissen huts for sleeping if one got time, there was not much free time to go into the town of Dunoon to see what's about, one morning bright and early Pete and I my partner in claim and crime and trouble got up at 5.30 from guard and took a walk along the waters edge, we saw a full box of jaffa oranges and a large tin of biscuits, we carried our loot back to the S.P's and huts we split the case up between our pals just getting up, when beds were made up it was a job to hide them, in coat pockets, gas caps in blankets, but beds looked lumpy, cause the old Sgt Major Lang started to poke around and hidden fruit appeared so it spelt trouble. When the duty officer came in he was told about our little find so he told the BSM to punish those responsible so where he found oranges were the ones to loose their half day in Dunoon so Pete Black, Ack Jarvis, Eric Wells and me were given the task of moving 105mm shells to another dump, he lost his half day too cause he had to be there.

Our invasion practice over we got ready to go back to Motherwell and a scheme out to Peebles common covered in heather until we messed it up. Crossing the ground two of them started sink in us they weighed 28 ton. They were soon in trouble to get out of it. Four really in trouble the drivers tried to reverse which it worse, he sent me in to put tow rope on F2 and we were lucky to get F3 out, while F4 was further out and still sinking by the time L.A.D arrived, F1 was well down they put a double rope and winched it slowly, gunners dug at the rear, 8 foot down about 6 inches above ground level, it was spoken to abandon it, but the answer Danny got was get it out. It was an all night job. Good old Danny. I think he got a choke off for that.

The next game was to teach the sergeants how to drive and handle the S.P in case the driver came to grief, so one day I said we would use Glasgow Road, doing nicely until we came face to face with a trolley bus, he couldn't move over, the sergeant did a panic on the side pavement good job there wasn't a kerb lifted, having seen a bit of the town, we would get on the road back, good hill appeared which he didn't like with a big drop one side, they slide very easily n cobles, he stopped and said you take this down unless you want to see inside the hospital.

Our old Colonel Major Kay Lewis (handle bars) to 49 said he would get this lot from here before xmas, he did to a place Waberswick in Suffolk. We came down S.P's on transporters followed by the light vehicles and motorbikes, we had a break near Cambridge, I volunteered to give the signal N.C.O a break, there was a motive for that. When we came to the tisby corner I had other ideas I stopped there with the officers Lt Kirby also stopped there with me, he must have read my thoughts. My other brother stood on the Westley X roads.

We pressed on one lad got a puncture and stayed the night at Bury Brks it was when we got to our destination house near the sea. Our guns arrived later so we drivers had to go a mile back up the road to some old buildings I took the bike but the blessed thing ran out of petrol. I left it there after we drove the S.P's across the heath into the wood and walked back to the village. The time was just gone 0100 when I laid my sleeping bag down, next day march one mile each time, they had some real deep tank traps to have a go in, a new crusader tank that was smashing to drive but it would not get out of the trap it was to low the S.P pulled it out, it was fun to lump down in the bottom and crawl up one minute you see the clouds, next few minutes down again. Our guards on the S.P's at night was a bit creepy with a few adders crawling around, we used to sit on a bank under a fir tree and watch for the orderly officer to come so we could stop him, if he thought we were going to walk round inside the wood.

We had time to get used to them when the W.O. decided to get us back on 25 pounder guns. There was only about 10 people living in the village a load of old snobs to put it bluntly. I got time off for xmas day, the first time we had all been at home for several years, Danny B gave me a pass just for the day, not to leave the billet before 0700 am. Xmas morning I left the house where we were billeted around 5am and walked to Saxmundham, a person pulled up and gave a lift for a mile, so I don't know where he had been at that time of day, my brother knew some people there who had put a bike beside their house for me also a diagram of the villages. I would pass through on my way to Stow market and the main road to Bury and on to Risby, I made it at ¼ past one in time for a rest and 55 miles. Before lunch was finished an American fighter crashed in a field near the apple store. The bullets were going everywhere.

I left for my return trip 3pm taking my bike with me, I left the Dorsham station rode my bike and pulled the other to Saxmundham back to the house and thanked them very much and rode off in darkness and freezing weather. I asked across the road if I could put my bike in his garage, oh yes said the man three days later he told our Sergeant Major that it was in his way and wanted it taken away so I kept it in the cellar of the house until my next ride to Risby, which was quite often.

We did all water proofing of our vehicles here what a game it was each Sunday a run to Gorleston swim pool to test, it came in quite high 6 foot I sat on a 4 gallon square can but I still sat in water no excuses, when the jeep went down the ramp one N.C.O sitting on top rolled off into the drink, pity it wasn't our Sergeant Major that would have raised 3 cheers, that made a days outing.

We left Waberswich in February for Cromer where we were in residence at the hotel metropol none paying guests most of the front was wired off, here we did more training, we come to the Stanford Battle area and would stay maybe a week of ten days, when firing smoke I went to pick up the nose caps off the shells clean varnish off and down the cellar at the hotel gas was on, they were made into ash trays, polished them up soldered a badge on took them to the tea shop round the corner, in that day lot nice ladies ran the shop.

On one occasion going to the range a 15 cwt burnt its coil out, so I said to the Sgt Major Lang lend me your bike I can get one in Bury, he must have read my thoughts, oh no I will take you, so it was home I knew we had one in the garage while I found it he was talking to my parents, it was dark and cold, when we were ready to go the old bike wouldn't start, so pop had to give it a push. We duly arrived back to fit the coil and drive the truck back, nobody liked him especially me on one scheme some of the motorcycles were going in a competition so I had the job to check his bike over, I saw to it he wouldn't win or even finish the coarse, he tried to find out who did his bike but nobody knew. Somebody did I reversed his twist grip so it had to be twisted anti clockwise for more revs, and half a turn on the carb needle.

We had a large heap of sand for practice so he thought he was good while he was talking, a rope was tied on the carrier just to let him get nearly on top, the rope pulled tight so his rear wheel ground in, and clever clogs was sitting on top stuck fast and all help had disappeared as one would expect for a snide like him.

All the main body of our Regt 143 Field sign the polar bear they were the first wheeled guns into France, I was left at Cromer a bit longer with a spare tower (quad) and two limbers fully loaded inside and more on top one 15 cwt was loaded with spares. The driver for this truck took it for a run along the front at Gorleston, was soon picked up by the M.P's and brought back, so an officer from the other BTY of our lot kept an eye on him when we next moved nearer to Gravesend. While we were being paid in Franc's the doodle bugs were landing not far away, it was mid afternoon on the 6th June Day.

They didn't want us just yet, as they had got many thousands on the beach to break out, hit old jerry hard and win, as many supplies would be needed in about seven days, the main regiment were there getting a foot hold, many tanks had run out of fuel and were caught, so we were put down off part of the mulberry harbour, on to sword landing beach making our way to a field where we had to remove some of the water proofing from the valve cover, distributor, petrol pump, tank petrol and engine. Before moving on to try and find our wagon lines in the dark, poor old Fenwick my driver said he was scared stiff at the harassing fire they were all colours and in all directions. Having gone on with my quad we stopped at a road junction to look for our sign, a Sgt Major came up, he said if you don't get this bloody thing moved they are shelling every ten minutes, that scared my driver a bit more for a start, so we pressed on regardless in the dark. We did about eight miles getting a bit weary decided to park in for the night in a field somewhere in France.

13 June having spent a quiet night sleeping in the quad with ammo around us, we had our rations for breakfast at 0700 ready to push on if my driver Femwich will be ready and willing, our breakfast was our camp ration one small cube placed in the dixie added small amount of water and watch the magic rise to give a dixie of porridge heated up inside on a meths stove, just the job. When it got lighter to see four ambulances parked under trees on the side of this field, but me driver wouldn't go to ask where our wagon lines were, they said they were attached to our lot, 49 Division and said the church with a hole through its roof, turn left your wagon lines are there we had made it but no sign of the 15 cwt. Just had time to get out and look around when BTY Captain came with my next job.

Was to take over a new Bren gun carrier to replace one that came to grief and its driver went bomb happy, and ran over a mine, saw no more of him, a quick start so my afternoon was taken up by filling sand bags and on the floor and seat of the carrier. During the afternoon a jerry plane came over firing, one lad Bill Smith started to run, but a bullet hit his rifle slung over his shoulder and bent it over to make a good walking stick, it paid another visit, spotted the quads under the tree. Ron Usher was inside writing a letter to his wife, when a 20mm cannon bullet came through the roof and his writing pad, between his legs and out the bottom into the ground, I said he was going to dig it out. I saw a real welcome to this village in Rauray.

I got to work to find a shell box to bolt on the front for rations I didn't get time for anything before my crew of two signallers and one officer Danny Brabin o.p, said you will be driving this tonight with four more carriers to a new position we will follow and tank tracks of deep ruts full of water, no lights and pitch dark about seven miles. At around 0300 hours one clot got his track off, he had dozed off, Danny said you stop and help him, I said it's up to him to put it back on, I've got no rations either and these others have tools so I went back and told him to wait till it was light, he was a bit cheeky, so I had some rations with the others and he was left to fit it, he was told to get his spade and break the side of the rut down, to wind it back on, one of the others told him to stay awake next time.

It was a dodgy old run the nest position when jerry gave us another look dropping poisoned sweets and small tablets of soap just wash the hands and bang no hands. While the o.p officer was looking for a target smoke from a gun barrel gave the game away.

I sat on a tree stump making a cuppa it wasn't minutes before we had some attention, a shell landed very close, I couldn't hear anything for about an hour. The officer had used the rope ladder that gerry had left and he lit a torch to read his compass. There was a field of wheat I just walked in a little way and to my surprise the tail of bomber sat there complete, and the gunner still on to his gun, I told Danny he said go through his pockets for identity, then bury him.

This o.p at Demouville where some of tanks ran out of fuel or knocked out and the crew were trapped inside, and being consumed by huge black and yellow beetles. I got in and tried to get a bren the stench was too much to hang about. The gerry had scattered their kit everywhere, just further across this adjoining field a German half track also knocked out while I was getting a blow lamp out of a locker a big shell disturbed me somewhat, I took my loot and returned to the hedgerow for safety.

This petrol blowlamp wonderful it did all cooking for us four who nearly lived on the carrier, but officer changed each week. I only saw the Q.M for a few ration like tin bacon, tea, sugar and powder, all mixed in, perhaps old hard tack (biscuits) some rice, and tin fruit but mostly fresh fruit was plentiful after a visit to a garden for eggs and a pullet or two I think. I looked after men well we didn't starve.

Caen 7.7.44. In July was very hot spot more ways than one, we lost another scotch lad who was sitting on the step of the quad writing a letter when a tiny piece of air burst penetrated his heart that fatal. Our o.p here was an old building. We had some good kills round here, as I drove past the end of a large wood I counted 50 Sherman tanks knocked out in the field and 4 88 German tanks which were dug in but they were sorted out. We were able to get to the side of the wood and get the last one, we had the advantage of being low and not always seen. The town was very much bombed by the RAF, we had little time to spare so Pete and I went across a field to see what we could borrow to make use of, a sewing machine came back with us, no rations found here we didn't go to far in or hang about, not much change from maconeque, that was meat, spuds, peas and gravy.

This was our Christening into the militia and to the mud dump of Oswestry. To march in mud and expect clean boots for 8am parade. Instead of drilling

Oswestry – these four lads are about for off draft to the 3rd Infantry Div. can't be worse than here. To have a wash one has to walk through a small lake.

A small group of Tunbridge-Wells billet an old jam factory. Every morning a mile to march to the drill-hall of Southboro. The vehicles there were a load of clapped out cars and trucks.

This was Easy Troop waiting to Cross the Rhine by pontoon bridge at Wesil erected by the R.E.s (Royal Engineers) for the 147 Essex Yeomanry. The officer: Capt. Vance - he was one of the lads.

WAR MEMOIRS 1939-1946

This photo was taken in Iceland at Alafoss - the place where our camp was. At this spot boiling water comes up at all times, day and night. This water was transported down to Reykjavik by insulated pipes in a concrete tunnel.

To celebrate the King's birthday most of the soldiers were brought to parade along the 2 miles of concrete road built by the Germans prior to 1940. On the left is Sir Winston Churchill.

This is a model of an S.P. (Self Propelled Gun) – fires 25 pound shells can be AP Armour piercing or NE and up to 16 miles on super charge. Had I made it in steel then it would have gained a first. The engine was a 9 cylinder radial aero engine rather expensive to run 5 gallons per mile, 28 mph flat out.

Here we have the real S.P. Gun firing several rounds for the Germans. The driver is well down by the side of the gearbox which is quite large. The empty shell cases of brass are collected later.

WAR MEMOIRS 1939-1946

This was my Co. D. S. Hamilton 1ˢᵗ World War soldier. I was chosen as his driver for 2½ years. He was a good man, strict but fair. We kept in contact after his demob. I used to go and see him. I committed the top crime anyone in uniform could do and he got me out of that – my transfer by the W.O. 156 days detention at Woolwich.

This photo is of Qud Limbere Gun at their Camp at Baldurshagi, that was about 5 miles from Reykjavik, they were preparing to go out on gun practice. In the winter ones hands stick to the metal. One year the hospital ship called at Akureyri in the north and got frozen in.

Back to Iceland and how the Nissan were down piled half way up with rocks and lava dust, on one occasion we had a gale in excess of 100 mph. The gun towers and their winch ropes were placed over the top to hold them down. We had M.G. practice with an old Lewis years old.

This was the end of my travels, a salute was taken by General Dempsey G.O.C. to the 2nd Army. That took place on the main road into Hanover. He came to the lads and shook hands with some of them. In civilian life he became a director of Greene king.

WAR MEMOIRS 1939-1946

Here is Mr & Mrs Dai Thoma and son Melvyn now a retired Head School Master of a large school in the Midlands. I first knew Mel as a school boy of 10 when our Regt. moved to the village of Penclawd. He brings his wife Ann to see us in Bury St. Edmunds.

BATTLESHIP EAGLE HAS LANDED DIVERS £15 MILLION JACKPOT

by Ron McManus

DIVERS have salvaged the six-foot bronze imperial eagle from the German battleship Graf Spee — and they could be in line for a share of £15 million.

That's how much the huge bronze eagle weighing nearly half a ton is expected to fetch at auction.

The Graf Spee was the pride of Hitler's fleet, but Captain Hans Langsdorff scuttled her in the sea off Uruguay in 1939, rather than risk the ship being captured by the Royal Navy.

Soared in value

Divers had to loosen 145 bolts holding the eagle to the stern before bringing it to the surface.

The war may be long over, but interest in memorabilia from those dark days has never been higher and items associated with the conflict are now fetching extraordinary prices.

An all-in-one boiler suit with a pinstripe pattern, designed and worn by Churchill during the war, sold for £25,000, and a record £235,000 was recently paid for a VC won by an RAF airman who saved his Lancaster bomber.

But everyday World War II items are also now much sought after.

Many servicemen returned from the war with a souvenir or two, and those mementos have soared in value over the last 50 years.

For instance, a genuine-issue Home Guard belt is now worth £45.

A wartime German officer's hat could fetch at least £400, while a German mountain trooper's soft cap could fetch a cool £500.

German forces in wartime wore a vast range of metal badges on their fighting uniforms, and they were often taken as souvenirs from captured soldiers, sailors and airmen.

But today, a "close combat" badge is worth around £500, and a "wound" badge, of which thousands were issued, should fetch £50.

The value of Allied memorabilia is also increasing. An RAF flying helmet should fetch £200, and even a genuine British army vest is valued at £20.

And tens of thousands of British servicemen kept their old army-issue leather jerkins when they were demobbed.

Back in the 60s and 70s, they were a familiar sight being worn on building sites and allotments, but their value has grown to £85.

Ever wanted to touch an H-Bomb?

AN "H-bomb" has gone on display for the first time, and is generating waves of interest.

The thermo-nuclear device is part of a unique exhibition of man's destructive power at the Yorkshire Air Museum.

"Until the Berlin Wall came down in 1989, people lived and grew up with the constant threat of nuclear attack," said Museum Director Ian Reed.

"The H-Bomb (pictured on the left with staff member Christine Mellor) had a huge effect on a whole generation, yet virtually no-one has ever seen one.

"For younger generations, this is only history but now, for the first time, you can see — and touch — a nuclear bomb in this new display."

With a 400,000-tonne yield, the WE 177 bomb was 30 times more powerful than the device used at Hiroshima and Nagasaki in 1945.

First delivered to RAF Cottismore in 1966, it was fitted to aircraft such as the Vulcan, Buccaneer, Jaguar and Tornado — some of which are also on display at the museum.

Britain's last air-dropped nuclear weapon, the WE 177 was withdrawn in 1998.

The Yorkshire Air Museum is situated on Halifax Way, Elvington, York, and is open every day from 10am to 3pm until March 26, after which it'll stay open until 5pm throughout the summer.

Flawed genius fled from Nazis to NASA

Von Braun in civilian clothes with Nazi top brass at the rocket research site at Peenemunde. And, below, one of his V-2 rockets.

Wernher von Braun made Moon landings possible — but he was also responsible for designing Hitler's dreaded V-2 rockets

President Kennedy pointing the way to the stars for Von Braun in 1963.

by Jim Montgomery

AS World War II drew to a close, a race began between America and Russia to capture Germany's top rocket scientists.

America narrowly won what Churchill called The Wizard War, to harness the expertise of boffins like 33-year-old Wernher von Braun.

During the subsequent Cold War, he was to play a huge part in the US v Russia Space Race — to put the first man on the Moon.

The United States won; again, largely thanks to the visionary German rocket-man and wartime SS Major who became "The Father of America's Space Age".

Arrested by Gestapo

Having invented the wartime V-2 rockets that caused havoc in London, Von Braun later designed the Saturn V that in 1969 helped make Neil Armstrong the first man to set foot on the Moon.

A new book, *From Nazis to NASA* tells the story of Wernher von Braun's remarkable determination to turn his boyhood dream of manned space travel into reality.

A Prussian aristocrat — his father was a Baron — young Wernher was a child prodigy.

At the age of four, he could read a newspaper upside down, and by the time he was 12, he'd built his first rocket.

Aged 15, he read a science-fiction story about a trip to the Moon, and decided that here was "a task worth dedicating one's life to".

That's just what he did — in 1930, he prophetically declared, "I bet you that the first man to walk on the Moon is alive somewhere on this Earth".

Thousands of miles away, Neil Armstrong had just been born.

The German army soon saw the potential of rockets, and Von Braun worked for them before Hitler came to power.

The gifted scientist used Germany's awesome military machine to advance his rocket-building dream.

But after he was arrested by the Gestapo and accused of having his heart set on space and not on destroying London, it took the intervention of Hitler to have Von Braun released.

Near the end of the war, plans were afoot to have German U-boats launch rockets on New York, and a variant of the V-2 was to have wings, a pilot and landing gear.

As Germany crumbled, Von Braun surrendered to the American army, and tried to keep his rocket team together.

Historic

Eventually, he led 117 rocketeers out of the devastation of defeated Germany to America, in pursuit of making manned space flight possible.

However, controversy over Von Braun's past dogged him.

Hollywood's 1960 movie biography was entitled *I Aim At The Stars*, which led comedian Mort Sahl to add, "but sometimes I miss and hit London".

Many now forget that Russia was well ahead in the Space Race when in May, 1961, President Kennedy committed the goal, before this decade is out, of landing a man on the Moon and returning him safely to Earth".

The first historic lunar footsteps eight years later wouldn't have been possible without Wernher von Braun.

His early death, aged 65 in 1977, just before the advent of the NASA Shuttle, robbed him of his ambition to travel into space himself.

But he'd already achieved his boyhood dream — he'd made it possible for Man to walk on the Moon.

His tombstone reads simply, "Wernher Von Braun 1912-1977 Psalms 19:1".

This passage referred to was his favourite: "The heavens declare the glory of God: and the firmament showeth his handiwork".

● *From Nazis to NASA by Bob Ward, is published by Sutton at*

This is one of the V2 of which England had a lot. By the look of the people at its base it could be 30 feet. This was our last target before being disbanded. I was stuck on a bridge that was sinking and mines below, being lifted off in the morning and linkage checked. I had 25 miles further to a Canadian pontoon, then through the night until 12pm next day to the OP for target. Danny worked out the timing from what the RAF gave one or two Air Burst and he did the job. We went up to see the result. Good.

Newspaper Extracts © The Weekly News D.C.Thomson&Co.,Ltd

Holoville was a small village we had a job here of gerries hiding in slit trenches they had dug in a field of turnips, some gardens produce was ripening up tomatoes made a nice change, not much bread but plenty of hard biscuits. We didn't have arms in the carrier to take this lot as we only four and the o.p officer was Danny being a barrister he always told me no stealing, he didn't always know where his food came from, we always had clean plates not tin ones, here waited for the infantry to come who we radioed for, ten minutes later six lads came with auto's a few rounds were let off, some German shouted to them to give up and another ten were taken prisoner and marched off. We continued to our o.p to call for a couple of airburst over the area. This observation post was a church in Pondulamere where this week was Lt Mervin Brown the officers changed over each week I didn't have a change as our troop had lost two carrier drivers for this job so they had to enjoy my cooking and to supply our food, often we only saw the Q.M perhaps once a week, but we did alright. Chicken supply here was good eggs to plenty, we are now getting in an area where many houses were empty and people gone, I scout the places out to see what I can borrow. Melvin Brown was a good boy to be with not fussy like Danny.

8th August still in this area but going to a fresh position, by what I am told a bit on the bright side, a sniper was coming with us from D.L.I's infantry. H.Q so about 11pm I had instructions what was on to drive along a narrow lane with Danny walking along side holding his white handkerchief up, so I should not go on the grass where mines are placed, roughly 300 yards along this track, I turned hard 90 degrees right through a shallow ditch and into a potato field, go slow to prevent my tracks hitting the top 100 yards. Turned 90 degrees left to cross the ridges, near a gateway we turned into an orchard, here our sniper left us for his part.

I drove through the apple tress to a huge ramble bush in the corner, we stayed there three hours in the middle of these prickles, no cooking only hard tack. Three (3am) Danny called our guns for six rounds air burst they whistled over us as they had not much further to go before they did their job. 0040 four further rounds of H.E went on the farm buildings containing many more Germans an early wake up for them. All kaput by now 9am.

By 0900 hours I backed out from our hide having a walk round where we came in to see trip wires running through the grass up and down the apple trees to a board near where we came in, they had tied twelve grenades to a board, so I cut all wires and stood the board up in the corner, was a nice summer house, probably some gerries were in there when we came in, as they left a tin hat and three mugs. I guess we had disturbed them.

Now this was a little bit gruesome we went to see what the results were I wanted a pistol as I had plenty of ammo for it, I saw one in a slit trench on a Sgt Major he had an arm missing, so I said to Jimmy Russell a wireless operator in the carrier, give me a pull with him, he said I cant do that. So I took a rope and placed it gently over his head, and under his stump hopped in and drove forward and gerry object. So I got one prize, Danny saw two officers brown polished jackboots as he was running but no way could we get them off. That was very good saved my skin twice as later on it played a big part.

Le Harve we took part in one or two villages before this big port, one afternoon we laid in orchard and watched a thousand bomber raid go in, I think it was such a wonderful sight I must say but not for those receiving it. Danny often got lost but was good on ranging. He couldn't hit a rabbit with his pistol, it sat there waiting for another one. But he could land on target very well with big stuff. We paid a visit to several villages on the way to Le Harve, in the afternoon we got short of rations no time to go back for any here we met our infantry company who we were going in with in the morning at dawn, we cruised around in order to find a good place to sleep. I stayed in the carrier all night, about 0130 hours I got the blow lamp going on kerb and fried some tin bacon, and a cuppa, I went to wake up the three, Danny said he had been out twice to see if I was alright. I laughed at that. Anyway we loaded up and drove down to the dock area to meet 600 hundred gerries marching out, children walked with them kicking them. An infantry officer shouted to me to get the bloody off the street they are lining up an 88, I moved quickly at that time of morning.

I went back to our lot for more rations and mail and away again to support the D.L.I infantry they were going to clear a village. We were to meet them at noon and the church hill tanks, had been in and cleared them, they went round we had to sit in the vehicles and wait, it was raining we had no cover on the carrier. I got out to stretch my legs, there was a house by the roadside and a garden, so as I walked up the path. I hadn't gone too far when a 88 high velocity shell passed me I felt the wind from it, what the hell was that. I very soon went back to the carrier no stop for tomatoes just that was too near for comfort. I had to stay here the night with my crew and company of the Durham light infantry (DLI). The night turned out to be quite thrilling we had a late tea at 7pm, settled down in a house with the lads for the night, they formed a guard on theirs and our vehicles on the roadside about 9.30 the C.S.M came in and asked for a patrol of six, no problem they jumped with their autos and away about two hours later heard firing not far away. I had a nights sleep and breakfast at 7am at another house, as we left, where slept and passed the front lawn a dead gerry laid there they raised his arm to salute Hitler, his loss. After this little dig we left and went on our way.

We left the D.L.I's to get another section where our assistance was a long run I think however we had wide river to cross, I thought it the Seine not sure. I got there in early evening to lead our guns across and away to find our OP for this target. The bridge was the railway that was sinking after an explosion charges had upset things for me, I got a little way on with mines at the side of the track, a piece of steel came up and caught the linkage so I was stuck there for the night. The guns got by me but one 15 cwt got off the line its equipment was to another and then pushed in the drink. I had to sit in the carrier all night, in the morning the L.H.D came and lifted it up off the steel plates and taken into workshop to check the rods underneath. I was there until 3pm during this break I had a poke around this place, they had placed a few pressure mines here. I found plenty of 9mm bullets of which I had a few boxes ready for use, when I got the ok to go we had to travel a further 25 miles to cross on a pontoon bridge, it was flat out then to make up time all the rest of that day all night till 12 next day we had one stop to change a bogie wheel the tyre had gone, so while I changed that the lads made a brew up.

Our target was a rocket site underneath large beach trees our o.p called for airburst shells and four rounds of H.E went up to see the remains of the place twelve bods had taken rest on the ground. The shed holding two more rockets had walls fourteen inches thick of concrete one more on the tail ready to launch to England.

That place was called Peeromande somewhere in Belgium while going the towns we were limited to only a few shells on military targets so we didn't knock Holland or Belgium about much, we had a little rest before next venture of being dragged through trees about five foot high, after losing a track and could feel the trees pushing the plates up as I was pulled a Sherman backed up and pulled me out of the planton. Soon as I was clear ground Danny went off on the tank leaving Geo muggings to break the track and replace it and watch which way they went, that was a task to try and follow track marks on enemy country, no fruit or chickens in this poor area Arras.

The people along were pleased and gave us apples and plums we passed through the village St Hubert a lot of small farms most fowls running around had I thought eggs would help out box. We had a break, while waiting for our infantry to turn up also we were looking for a nice empty house for the night. Bed and breakfast free our o.p always looked for a large house or somewhere on high ground. I took his valise in and the wireless operators, but I slept in the carrier I had a gerry bayonet sharpened to good knife and my right hand held my pistol inside my battle dress, at 0130 hours I woke up the inside sleepers for a cuppa on the pavement before going on down the road all eyes open, when an officer shouted to get that bloody carrier off the road they are lining up 88 gun. I very quickly good reverse and by side of a house and watched the infantry marching them out to swell the prisoners by 800 some of the officers carried pyjamas on their arms, they didn't look happy.

Linought getting along here we were going out with the recce group lads to go on one of their forward roads, they had armoured cars the leading car, then we followed in case things required something bigger. The leading car saw the enemy in a field trying to escape, and opened fire with his 20mm canon. He was knocking them down like ninepins. One infantry carrier went in and a gerry hiding on a grass stack jumped in the carrier to get the driver. I sat tight enjoying the fun, soon eight more tried to get away to the road but the officer spotted them and soon they were laying flat., they fell like skittles. A shallow ditch ran along the road where one gerry was getting a bazooka lined up on us, but the officer spotted him and opened fire down the ditch and shot ten more medical bod's. To my surprise an armoured car appeared out of the wood who should get out but my Col Hamilton, so he and Danny were having a chat, while I watched a live medic going along giving a white tablet to each they all had a good hole in their stomach. The medics should not have been armed as I stood and watched one he said comrade. I answered him I had an eye his Kriegmarine watch, but Danny said come on Gamble let's go he will shoot you, I just said I don't think so.

On returning to our bty for rations I saw a lorry which had a nice cover on it, but not for long as my blankets could do with some cover so I borrowed one piece of it to make a sleeping bag for myself, laying it open on the ground and laid on it myself with a piece of chalk allowing for a wrap over and enough for jacket etc at the top when the chance arrived, when I got a chance, next came some straps to fasten it.

Well our next little trip was through a mangol field and had to wait for a tank to pull us through as mines had been planted and tanks tracks were to deep for the bren carriers. This led us to Rosendal, before town we had a position in a village where the o.p officer had changed to Lt Mervin

Brown he was easy going, he saw a wind mill to look out on german positions, there were several people sitting in the bottom of the mill for safety. I had been round the garden and collected up tomatoes and eggs and six pullets, I soon stretched their necks and in the box, a few minutes later an infantry officer wanted the o.p officer so I had to call him down, and we were to advance into Rosendal. So driving along Mervin was already plucking fathers and covering the lads marching behind.

This was quite a large town and a railway centre, factories, sweets, sugar factory and others as we would be here Mervin went to a cottage and asked the lady if his men could sleep in a down stairs room, yes that alright I will go next door to my friend so and a lovely coal fire in the kitchen was just the job of roasting the pullets. It was everything I would need there, the other two signallers rested. By the morning all was well four thanks to our Dutch lady, leaving one behind for her kindness. We left to join the lads in the rail yard after setting up the blow lamp and oven we had chips and fried onions with our pullets, we invited Danny to join us for lunch he consented, he said when he saw what his lot had got was just fried spam. For afters we had rice pudding and condensed milk, that was when he asked some questions. I told him to ask Lt Brown. I feed my crew on the best available.

Weert had a nice canal running quite close to where we had our position was in a farmyard for the officers of the three bty's they went forward by Sherman tank to do a recce, we had a good look round to make sure we had no company in hiding, it wasn't long before they landed one at the wall of the old building in which I sat writing a letter, they store a lot of corn straw up top, this one had barley straw and harns and husks came down and covered me while I was doing my notes up. They must have seen us go in since we had more shells, more holes and more muck. The officers were gone all day expected to be back at 7pm and expected to take food so in the afternoon another shell landed and killed a bullock not far into the field. I knew the ration box was getting low, so taking a look at the situation decided to take my sharp knife to have four nice steaks of the rear leg, before that took place I was warned off by another shell close, crawling back under cover of a bank to wait around, 5pm I triad once again ok four nice slices were duly cut so I crawled back getting some spuds to cut up for chips. While the two bods kept look out just in case we might get other visitors.

I got the lamp going and fry pan on the go and the oven to keep the plates hot, not our turn to wash up no problem washing up just take clean plates from previous houses, anyway we had our fed which was by we three. The chief come right across and said don't cook much Gamble that looks fine, so he took it over to the other officers they looked at his and said where did he get that nice piece of meat? Good question. Danny asked I said the village butcher called, oh no! There is nothing in the village look sir we have had three big shells landing quite near one killed that bullock. Oh no he said. I went and looked at the barges on the Weert canal and spent the evening inside by a grate fire, it was lovely and was quite roomy.

While I was running around Holland we had a new C.O take over when we were at Penclawdd in Wales this was the first time I had seen them his name McKay Lewis handle bars to us 2 inches each side, one day very hot a mobile shower had been set up with a 45 gallon barrel in an apple tree, his new H.Q. was a large mansion with a long drive leading in, about ten of our lads sat on a wagon shaft waiting, but not being used to him and falling debris, I stared at his convoy leading one motor, a jeep, and a truck and two motor bikes. When started to round the bend the lot came to a halt, my hat sat on the back of my head watching them still he shouted and beckoned at me to go to his jeep. He said what do you think this is a bloody menagerie show 11am the Colonel of the 185 field Regt, what's your Regt I told him 143 field regt. Go back and separate, an incoming plane could shoot the lot of you only one thing was missing the old monkey of cause. We had a lovely shower on a hot day to lay the dust many tracks were the answer to drawing shell fire once gerry spotted dust rising up over a field he would often follow it with a few big ones.

Blerick here we were sleeping in a wood Danny said it might be a rough night I said don't you think it a bit daft when you saw what our air burst did to the wood near Le Harve, but we still dug his slit trench for him and put his valise in, I said we are parked beside the carrier the soil was very light so when the big boys opened up the ground shook and soon voices were heard coming from the trench, help me! Help me!. The sides had caved in on him we looked at each other and said shall we go? Yes! He had his hands inside and straps over so he was well and truly stuck, had it been our bty Sgt Major he would have had to scrape himself out, after that night shells passing over, we drove along to Venlo still in Holland I think we came to a bridge where R.E's were putting new one over, we stopped as he spoke to them, they said they don't stop here we have lost about five yards on a shell landed right behind us it lifted the carrier right up on its nose. The cobles came down just behind us, pulling of the road into a cottage garden another one landed just in front of us, the clods of soil this time, but the gerry was knocked out, as we proceeded on our way to witness the attention of the RAF by machine gunning a big column of Germans and horse drawn guns and wagons, some parts still smoking. One 3-ton lorry I saw had been captured at Dunkirk and used as a vets section for the horses, many had been shot by the RAF's visit and in a ditch laid dead, not a very nice sight to see all those lovely horses.

Our next village had a windmill which Danny used as look out, he went up the top where gerries had knocked a brick out to watch our progress across the fields and other places, my next job was to go up to do the same, make a hole in the wall only sixteen inches through. A good chisel and hammer took most of the afternoon and evening. I left the last one remaining brick until dawn next morning, had gerry seen that go out he would have sent out a shell at the hole, as I down the many steps, on a seat at the back sat a gerry asleep, I had a word with Danny and warned when he came down, he said you don't need telling what to do, so my pistol had to do the job for me. When I came out to the carrier stood a man trying to make the signaller understand that fifteen were in a cellar at the end house.

The signallers contacted the infantry who sent two lads with auto's, where are they? So they gave them chance to give in, but no two bullets at the lock and put that, one gerry was shot by one of the others, they brought him out he was a big devil too. So we dug a big deep hole seven foot and plonked the pair of them in it, filled it made two crosses to hang their hats on, another job well done.

The German gun which was firing one shell every ten minutes, but that gave away its place because of smoke he could see nicely from my hole, it was a tank gun, dug in the ground with just its turret out and a large elder bush planted on its back to give it good camouflage. T night several of their tanks came to village shelter at a high fence for company, that was a big mistake, late at night the infantry paid a quiet visit they fire armour piercing shell which explodes into insides. They lost five tanks. Now around Venlo fruit quite plentiful, I just managed to rescue some plums and tomatoes and half a dozen nice brown eggs. Mervin was with us this week, he selected a house on high ground along a narrow road, but eyes spotted peach trees in a garden and they were loaded, I made up a tale to go down the road, some of them would go down a treat. My tale was that one of our old lot was on the other side of the hedge, but I didn't know that. Don't be long away the people were down their cellars laughing and talking little did they know someone was nicking their peaches. I climber up one tree and put them inside my battle dress jacket, while up the tree our guns opened up and the peaches fell to the ground, I came down pretty quickly as my feet touched the ground a company of Suffolk's opened up with bren guns dug under the fence, firing on a lot of Germans running across a field, and their smoke screen was lifting, loads of legs trying to escape not many did.

When I got back to the carrier a young man was trying to make one lad understand that the motorbike he had got there was his and the Germans had pinched it, when it ran dry they cut some wires and left it covered with straw, he said can you help me, no gas, no go. I tracked a few wires back and a bit in, put some gas in gave it a kick and away it ran. Can you give some gas to get me home to Belgium, so I gave him half a tank and had one ride on it, it was ozando machine hand change on the right side.

Sustern, after watching A/P shells dancing we carried on to a village near Sustern, shells had been coming over in plenty all sorts and sizes on one occasion by a group of Germans were standing by a vehicle one moved to go behind a bush, little did he know he was being watched and gave the others away. Danny called for a round of airburst which cut him short and nor for the others.

The night was spent in a house the o.p officer Danny and one wireless operator went in the house with him, but Percy the other one was with me outside, we dug a deeper slit than usual a shelling was expected. We entered a field through a squeaky gate and parked the carrier in a corner hopeful for a quiet night, we sat on a bank behind the carrier, the old gate was moved about 1.30am their time which gave us time to sit and get ready Percy with his sten, I fished my pistol from my battle dress pocket with sixteen tracers, loaded ready for who was coming to see what was in here or back way to the house. We could just make out what looked like three bod's heading down field our way, they were saying England yar yar Englander, one went Percy's side, two tried to open our box of rations on the front, bad luck mate.

They started to come, round the side where our deep trench was I sat ready for them, one received it and fell right in the trench so the other one heeded some more to make sure he wasn't pretending. Percy stopped his as he started to run, but he didn't get far.

It was a surprise for Danny to see our effort during the night. I wonder what he would have done. He tried to shoot a rabbit one day and it waited for another bullet.

It was our job before moving off to put no.2 in with mate and some soil over them to hold them in, and no.3 we left him where he went down. We didn't get any medals.

Around the village of Holden a big gun was shelling us and our o.p officer left us in a field while he went into a house to get bearings on it, and take it out. Danny called us his children another big one dropped and went off near us.

We dug our slit trench on the other side of the carrier, another shell came and exploded too neat for comfort, the shrapnel cut through two spokes sections of carrier bogie wheel, and broke the track in two places, it riddled Danny's valise, but he soon was able to take it out. We had some repairs to do before we could move on. Some of the crew he could see running about there before, we could move on another one, started he thought this could be tank come on the position. Danny thought what he was on he had a few more minutes grace, another one went to join him so Danny called for two rounds of airburst. That would be enough for the mission to be complete.

Before we got far another high velocity shell passed across the front of the carriers and hit the ground further on, a press photographer was walking down the hedge row but he soon changed his mind and direction and got behind a cottage, we got near this cottage so Danny went in and upstairs to get a better view. I pulled the carrier behind the back so it was out of sight to gerry, after about half an hour a different type of shell came, very near to us it blew a large hole in the wall of the house big enough to get the carrier through. We didn't see any more of the press reporters, more smoke to be seen so we left here and back to the wagon lines to get filled up more rations and collect our mail before setting out on our next venture.

Our next occasion we had a night drive following four Churchill flame throwers in action, giving them support in a creeping barrage if they needed it, behind the tank they pulled a frailer like a water bowser full of liquid phosphors at the press of a button and a jet of phosphors went out about twenty feet in front and burst into flames, they set fire to stacks, trees, building anything that night. This was a cold night but the heat which came back was terrific. A real sweat for us having to follow. The old gerries didn't like this medicine on a freezing night, the next day travelling along a piece of road which was frozen hard and a baron field saw armour piercing shells A.P just dancing up and down because the ground was to hard for them to enter a very good spectacular sight best not to be there on that piece of ground.

Limbeck I heard the Regt was going to be disbanded as Germans had more infantry than we had, some lads were worried as they had seen some of the conditions which the infantry come to terms with. One night several of the D.L.I's were nicely settled for the night, some of our lads were at the back of the house, it had a large conservatory with huge bunches of black grapes and nectarines all ready to be gathered in the morning before we four left, but around midnight an A.P shell came in through the front wall of the house over the heads of the sleeping D.L.I's and through the back it shattered all the glass and all the fruit laid on the floor damaged, so I had to leave without fruit but lives were safe.

Our gun position for that day and night was a dodgy old place, our Regt had been getting large dumps of ammo ready for a large barrage. Our lads did a guard on it during the day, and a Gerry patrol visit by night and made a sketch of the dumps when the guns came up the gerries were in the farm, tried to get away, our lads shot one, one was hiding in a straw stack, one lad saw straw move so he gave it a kick and a few bullets from his sten. They had a scout round in the hay loft where he was going to sleep, but another gerry was sleeping in the hay he shot Jim Russell then jumped from the loft into a waiting seven gunners so he got fifty bullets into him that was a bad place. They got him with the sketches, so they recovered the bulk of the shell dumps.

Not a lot just here for us to get, I did manage a few apples and tomatoes and few eggs and one chicken. Not a lot here to fill our ration box up, the night was windy, wet no lights to be used as our enemy was quite close. The smell from their clothes tells a tale that a patrol is about, perhaps laying a mine for us to run over, Danny couldn't make up his mind to go to the o.p or stay at this house as I was getting his valise of the carrier a big shell landed just in front of the carrier and the blast blew my tin hat off. I packed up the old tin hat and went into the house where an old man sat making up his cigars, when another shell came over the house very low, it didn't whistle as it should have done. The gun crew were just getting their bivi fixed up and making their cup of tea, one had put his cup on the tyre of the gun, this badly roamed shell fell into their bivi and killed four lads and two were very badly injured, as we were still there I had to give a hand to help the injured, one who his left leg just about off. The other had only been with us for about a month he still had English money which was shredded in his pocket.

Now moved on to near Coultral in Belgium one of the lads had some of their relations living in this village, he asked to go and see if they were still there, so the old Sgt Major took him on his motorbike. The planes were very busy the typhoons were after knocking out the tanks and wheeled guns, here on the next village Gits our other Bty was there one driver Peter Black was looking round, so we saw a large department store, it was packed with bottled fruit, cherries, peaches and pineapple sliced. Long shelves to houses lots more material, stamps and silks. Pete found a sack which we filled with as much as we could carry. I held the top on my back he took the bottom, as we were walking back slowly so the bottles and jars didn't break. A plane came over and dropped a dirty great bomb on the gas works across the road, Gee Wiz we broke into a steady trot but we made it. Lowe the Sgt Major asked where we got them, so he was given one to keep him quiet, a lot of activity round here just at that moment. The spitfire was about having a dogfight with German planes.

On the Sunday morning while driving the carrier and Danny as op officer saw the sky was black with planes all towing without any doubt, going to drop to capture the Arnhem Brigade but were sadly montgory dropped them in German armoured units hundreds were shot coming down and vehicles were damaged beyond use, around Limbeck Danny had gone with the Churchill tanks on a recce trip, it was eight pm return and Danny wanted his bed, so an officer and a driver with a 15 cwt to lead me up to where they were. All vehicles just had small white disc painted on the diff not much to see and keep in view so I lost sight of his truck the officer Lt Smith should have been standing up watching for the 7th armoured sign outside on the roadside, but as he was sitting down he missed a German patrol in the area, had turned the sign round, the lad with me spotted it we reversed as we went in the gate we saw the 15 cwt blow up.

Captain Brabin said is it Lt Smith, his truck has just blown up 100 yards up the road, he wouldn't believe me, but in the morning I passed it laying on the grass still smouldering, they tried to capture the driver they pushed him over the gate, and he ran for it in a ditch, the Gerri fired and the bullets passed through his epaulets in overcoat he laid in the ditch half full of water until the coast was clear.

The officer was taken in an ambulance somewhere? I went further up the road where Danny went to make some enquiries and a woman came out with a bottle of snaps, I had a glass of that which nearly bleeding choked me, just then three soldiers came on the scene looking for an officer and one man. I said we are ok it was one driver and one silly officer, don't know where he was taken to but we didn't see him any more.

Dec.16th. We find ourselves in Hanzan Belgium I think we are about to disband billed in private houses I was with a school master later Peter and Jimmy Russell joined us the owner gave us the front so if we left early he wouldn't hear us. We had a parade on the village square to say the enemy had more infantry than we had, so all gunners had been sent back to England to be trained as infantry. When they departed trades folk went to other unit regiments, it was dark and very cold. Pete Black, Jimmy, Charlie and myself went to menning and good entertainment, all free we stayed until 1am and got back at 5am ready to move to a town called Deschal, we parked on a disused glass factory, they used to make all green telephone caps for England, we had a break before going into Germany.

The river bridge had been blown, a wood platform had been put on the water so one could pull yourself across by the chain. Several people had gathered there including one R.E officer with a huge moustache and girls were taking the Mickey out of him, they beckoned us over to their home, their father was a manager of the glass factory. He said they had to go to bed early as they got one litre of paraffin per week, so big hearted Pete said he had got some, lets go and get it for them going to his truck to get it and put in a sand back, went back to the river crossing, they were very pleased with it. Dad came downstairs to thank Pete.

The girls Rolande and Georgette were both teachers in Brussels and come home at weekends. We had time to spare so went with them to the pictures and Mickey Mouse which broke down every five minutes.

The next day we had to move to Bourg Leopal with our vehicles we left them there and went by truck back to menning to stand by for another move, a lorry came ten lads taken for another regiment, so we had another free evening, went to an ensa concert.

Next day we were confined to billets not for long it was our turn to roll up blankets and put in the lorry for four hours ride, we picked up four signallers too but who was with the new lot, we soon found out. Before we parted company Danny did ask me if I would go back with him to the old Regt to be his driver again I thanked him very much but no thank you sir! I will have a change. Later a 3 tonner came for us on the way we learnt it was on s.p. lot 147 self propelled Essex Yeomanry.

Sat Dec 16th 1944. It snowed hard all day and residence being a large hole dug out with a tent spanning they had a stove in there, went well on borrowed coal. We had xmas on the 26th had an interview with the Bty Commander to find out what I had driven, I told him an o.p carrier, when our papers caught up I had a second visit to his office, he said I asked what you had driven you didn't say you had a course on these s.p's . There is a new one in the field you will drive that you will be in F Troop. We were soon given a job, Pete Black was posted to 413 Bty to drive 15 cwt truck.

27th December we were still in Cleve so an officer Captain Taylor wanted to go to Brunsam and back at 4pm, we went to Mastrick our dinner was at 5pm, our xmas day was put off ass a possible day for gerry to make attack, so dinner was very good taking it all round, turkey, fried spuds, apple sauce and port, plum pudding six cigars, fifty cigarettes and a lot of rum, some sweets and an orange.

That was that it was very cold and frosty went to Mastrick in the jeep, I got caught for a guard it was a quiet night next it was a visit to the m.o. for a medical most intake lads were there, that over, bed was next.

On the 30th December I was detailed to take Edgar to Mastrick dentist some teeth out. The roads were terribly bad I saw our old colonel Charlie Handlebars, he must have lost his job when 185 disbanded.

This Regiment had been fighting through from D Day onward to where I joined them in Hoenbrook where they were dug in a large pit with a tent stretched over, a stove also added to comfort, for outside we had deep snow this was the Ardens where Germans were making a final stand. The Americans were also there who were getting a real pasting from the gerries. We pulled out from Hoenbrook after another lot of snow, and the roads were bad on the way to Cleve we had a steep bridge to cross the crew got out to walk up, on the top the s.p turned broadside and slid down, to hit a house on the right hand side., when the last of eight hit it not much of the front wall was left standing.

December 31st. I was up 0450am to drive, first leave party to Reckmen the roads were really bad, I returned at 10am next day, soon after that they sent me with a 15 cwt wireless truck needing attention and we nearly got it from a low plane machine gunning the road along side us, this was time to get cover under a tree.

January 1st 1945. This day a call went out for all those with glasses to report to the m.o a truck was going to Enidhovvan for us to be tested for new spectacles. That was a long cold run in the back of a 3 ton Bedford.

January 3rd. In the morning it was getting the s.p filled up ready for the road, both tillers were frozen it was a job for my blow lamp to free. My no.1 Sgt was scared because the starting petrol pump was down there. It showed hard all day as we were moving through roads frozen one I slid off the road backwards down a bank and into an orchard, it was a job to get out, with no lights allowed another s.p got a direct pull across when on the road it was a gradual right turn.

January 9th. Our next position was in an open field joining a farm the crew had a look, cold and frosty I found the cowshed with twenty inmates having neck chains on hay made a good warm bed for me. But I hadn't thought of what happened at night, the crew had to stay with the gun and slept in a tent. They got a lot more sleep than I did the stench was terrible, enough but it plonk plonk and splash on the concrete. I was very glad when morning came, I went across the field a shell had burst near and pieces of hot shrapnel had burnt through the canvas and burnt the

Sergeants legs. The Q.M's truck wasn't so far away as he soon got a new pair of trousers, ready for leave to Susteron.

January 18th. It snowed hard we heard a lot of shooting went on the estate, German had put ten Polish prisoners into various cages, where they kept dogs we made a stop at this large place to let them go free they told and showed us where they had large stocks of guns twelve bores, they were hidden in wood crates all new, and buried beneath in paths we carried a steel spike on the s.p used for testing ground surfaces the lads would scout out for rations many of the people, buried food and clothes but found them.

Left here after five days of firing a lot of shells on the outskirts of Breman, I lost the tyre of my rear bogie wheel, it took about one hour to put a new one in, while I was doing this they were flirting with a Russian girl who had been a prisoner but had got out, but couldn't get back home yet. We drove on into the town more, it was a site to see after the large bombing raids. We left this area for Verden to put down a pocket of trouble on this place. We passed by the Belson entrance, here we pulled into a field for the night and in the morning he got out his manning minnies going at us, they got several 105mm shells in return, I was about to take a motor bike to bring up a ammo lorry, when a plane came over and let a bomb go it was meant for us. I stood near the gate and watched it right itself, I shouted to the others to take cover, it dug a good hole beside one gun, which saved us the trouble of digging. So I went on my way to get the ammo lorry, and then to go and borrow sheets from houses to cover the s.p, we would be moving back to Breman taking it my s.p started throwing out oil and covering one behind, so I had to pull on the side so the others to get by, two lads were due to go on leave so they were swapped with two from F3, we were left to be brought in by a transporter a big end packed up, being nine cylinder radial, it made real clatter driving it up. They took it right to work shops and I went with it, waited until the new on was fitted, they thought we were going to do their guards for them but the lad had another think. Here another move to Wollfeuch. Very noisy with a lot of shells coming in and going, about hundred rounds were fired one A.P (armour piercing) went into the sides of an s.p. gerry came over bombing. We moved to Heinbreng, got up about nine and a portion of bacon and liberate some coal and anything handy, took Rose the coal we went through. In Herbrick went to a house on the corner for a bath that was coal pay, (Emmas).

January 31st. Up at 7.30 and had a piece of bacon for breakfast, at 8am ready to move, 8.30 to Beek. Went down and back here it snowed all day at Geleen. Up about 8am and more bacon no eggs chickens didn't lay well here, back about 11am. Went to the troup at Warfersh in the noon and got a bike, flogged it for 20 gelders, got ready to move at 8 to a place called Mol, been here before at the glass factory. Pete and I went out and met Georgette and Rolanda went home, we had free time here some of the lads went to Bourg-Lepold, Pete and I went to the pictures to see Tarzan with the girls it was years old was about two when we got in and next morning up t 3am ready to move on again, this was a bad day. One driver got lost in a river I.S.P broke fire. So we got Enidhoven about eleven and civi billet.

February 7th. Got up at 8.40am and missed my piece of bacon, just got on parade to move at 1.30, put of until 4pm. Left Enidhoven and met the others on the road for tea, and waited until 12.45 before going on in the dark and landed at Nijmayen.

February 8th. At 5am started our guns a month, at sixty they put down a barrage with a large amount of tanks, went in the biggest barrage of the war, sleeping in the vehicle which the roof was leaking, stayed in village until dinner then moved to Aech at Nimogen in billets, got to bed at 2am after a good laugh with turkey face! Had some breakfast then took a UK leave patsy to Bourg Lepold a good long run 80 miles each way, the roads were very bad, got in bed at 12pm. Got up about 4am.

February 14th. Went to 30 Corp workshop with the old 15 cwt for new engine, rained hard all day long and plenty of doodles coming over.

February 17th. Not much done in the afternoon, the guns moved up to within 300 yards of him, a fly bomb landed in the next street and killed ten at 5.30, overslept due to the flea bomb changed the oil in the engine toHD30 and with a spot of cleaning, it came on to rain so we called it a day.

February 19th. Did a bit to the s.p had a cup of coffee went well by Nellie, rained most of the day, and at 7.30 we moved up again it was a long run this time.

February 20th. Had breakfast with the boys, we had easy day 800 rounds were fired guns, it rained most of the day and we had pancakes for tea by Ramsey.

February 21st. After breakfast it was a lovely day plenty of planes went over, he came over about ten and dropped a few bombs in the next fields to us went out in the jeep, and he came round again. Next day he paid us another visit to drop a few more, no shortage of planes up, went and saw Nellie in Nijmagen.

February 23rd. Rose about 8am had breakfast then to Brigade HQ, saw Major P Paul, it was not a nice day. The guns moved up to Goch at 1.30 had credit made up, carried on with the good work.

When I was done we had a long run to the north of Holland to help in capture of the Siegfried line. It was a real terrible place very deep mud, with no lights or talking was a job to get into ones position. Nearly 1000 guns and infantry took part, when the barrage ended the infantry went in and I saw one German come out, they had many first world war guns in the vast trench, hardly any leaves were left on the trees. The gun barrels got very hot and had to rest to cool. The laugh we had was that we had a Canadian pot bellied stove on board, this we had in the tent, that was lovely in there until the guard came in, said he smelt burning the poor Sergeant who laid near the stove his trousers were smouldering beyond saving, this was very cold, he only had half leg. The Canadians had skids fitted to their motor bikes each side that helped them to stay on in all the mud, that over now we can go back to Nienburg.

Taking a leave party one morning 26 lads in a 3 tonner going through a town quite slowly a German on a bicycle with no brakes came down a hill fast, he hit the back of the lorry bang, that was his lot for a while, a German saw it and came down, he broke one arm and a cut to his head, the copper said they were doing a lot to get into hospital for good food etc.

The police made a statement and signed it for me to hand in for my Bty officer. I had a 15 cwt and went to see him in hospital. The old boy laughed and said it was my fault, I will get a new bike with brakes a nurse came and translated what he said but I only went once.

March 14th. We had started to mass a large amount of equipment in a field close to the Rhine at Wesell, we were getting the s.p in position and the RE's were bringing the Rhine pontoons, in the evening we were getting ready to go on leave, that was put back a few days so before I was on guard with some more we were sleeping on the floor of a house ready to go on guard, I was near the door when a large shell hit the wall and covered them on the floor with dust and mortar, I was blown out the door much quicker than I wanted to, the blast lifted me up three steps to pick up my tin hat, I had three nights on guard before getting ready for leave.

March 15th. I got up at 6am and left Goch at 7.30am for Bourg-Lepold by truck, there at 2pm and food left at 6.30pm for Calais, we crossed the Rhine by train on pontoon bridge driven by RE driver. We had wood seats to Calais, 6.45 got tickets, breakfast and a rest, thick fog over the channel, the boat was absent off parade at 1pm. We left for Dover at 2.30 on the train for London 10.45 home.

March 19th. I got Gastroenteritis bedded until 10th April. I started on my return journey to Calais 10 hours, it was along hitchhike back to Genep, 10 hours. On another lorry ride.

March 23rd. Crossed the Rhine at night and were six miles in on a thirty-mile front, sorting out round Breman. They were at Lingen when I caught up with them, and we moved to put up our tent. It was a lazy day only 15 round to be fired, but he sent plenty back as the big bombers went to Bremen. Got up early had eggs and sausage for breakfast, but gerry gave us some airburst and injured 20 O.R's, the evening it poured with rain during our push for Breman. I got back to the guns on April 17th.

April 22nd. Moved 10 miles for another front near hay, after sleeping the night here we went to aid the 43rd Division, watched the bombers pound Breman. On the 26th was a lovely day for a fight, spent in a wood, and night moved to within 5 miles of Breman, up about 8am got breakfast filled up ready for the roads. The number one on our gun, he would share his naafi ration with the crew of his gun. This night I was laying on bed in a house on the floor of course, he brought half a mug of port. Knock that down and the other is a half whisky. I had most I couldn't get lower after an hour I had a good night, so I thought. I didn't know much about it, but at 5am the guard came and woke me. Get up at 6am, the cook is getting your breakfast, you are taking a leave party. I said I can't drive all that distance, so one of them drove it to Bourg-Lepold. I stayed on for the evening and something to eat before starting my ride to where I left them in the morning under the influence. No lights were allowed for night driving I called in at Nyjmagen and saw the people we had billets with when fighting that area. I was persuaded to stay longer until it started to get light. Then I came up behind a column moving about 5miles per hour, soon I could turn of from them and find my lot who had moved on a few miles, not bad 10.50.

May 3rd. Good day the Russians took Berlin we were going to move on at 12pm but this was cancelled as they were packing in two armies, gave into the yanks. On may 5th we all got a mug of rum, I put some of mine into a bottle for a rainy day. Dave a batman got his own back on a bombardier who nobody got on with Dave got a duck egg and threw it at the two tape head, and down he went. We pulled out at 6 after all to travel 60 miles to a place Nespapre many Russian women in camps.

May 12th. They started to clean up the s.p in earnest and also started p.t under Captain Taylor it didn't go down well, went out later with Frank and Fraulein. Had all day on the s.p ready for the C.O inspection, went for a walk up the G camp where the Russians were.

On Sunday 13th May we had no p.t all morning spent on the s.p and the evening for a church parade, tonight plenty of blanc, Monday came a big change in the weather was very cold to strip out for p.t at 6am. Poor little fellows, went on guard patrol and the Captain Taylor was a tall fellow one stride from him made three of ours.

More for he must think we were not fit by all this running about. Monday we had a violent storm passed the evening with a good fry up. When the rain eased up, Harry and I went to see what the fratting was like here.

May 30th. Still near Bramen going about 8 by transporter long run to Hanover, where we had P.O.W, to clean them to high level for GDC and the march past General Dempsey took the salute. The s.p we drove to park on an autoban with all the other track tanks side by side 18 miles patrolled by jeeps, so for now on it will be guards for us starting 5th may. We were doing a 24 hour guard and 22 girls bought in off the street causing disturbances, they went to the cellars and wanted a jimmy riddle every five minutes.

May 7th. Another grand day and the last for letter censoring, starting to go leave again to the UK, had another bad thunderstorm, very hopeful they are asking for volunteers for India.

9am Albert went on leave and we went on the move again to Hamburg, the weather was warm, that was our big town if they had not packed in, didn't stay very long as we were up at 4am and pushed on by lorry to Keil arriving there about 1pm and into some large German barracks, they had 13 main police stations before the war, by the bombing one could see right through, one end to the Keil canal, they sunk their fasted U boat here, each time it was lifted out of the water took fire, it had a lot of phosphors on board. We went out to see what we had come to, there was a 9pm curfew for the Germans, but when we returned to barracks, we had a big shock to see a German on guard for us at the entrance, a good job he spoke our language, he said that is good I guard you black hats.

Thursday 14th. Owing to these barracks being huge it was a job to find the showers it took most of the morning, in the afternoon we were to take a trip round the dock the Admiral Sheer and Hipp were here many more U boats, submarines, rained most of the morning went to a show in the evening. Sunday morning church parade you and you, were finished when we came out, but to get ready and polished up for a W.L Guard was a nice evening didn't go out, to much bull.

Monday 18th. Got up at 4am to go out 6am then had some breakfast rest until 10am then on again, the Brigadier came round and came at 6pm and went.

The day was very hot, as I mounted a 24 hour guard for WIK camp of P.O.W's from a window in another wing I heard my name called out, looking up there I spotted Darky Reid from my old regiment the 143 field they were off on demob, came off that one at 9am, and had the day off, took a walk to the town and a talk with a fraw who wanted to buy cigarettes, another guard for 48 hour, very hot day and old monty had to come to inspect the big ship Milwaukee changed over and went on the east gate, some of our navy lads were living on it. There was a small canteen on a small area for the navy working on the boats and raising the U boats, Sunk in the harbour. I went one morning as I traced the smell of coffee, when a bearded man said hello, don't I know you, it turned out to be an old school pal Donald Slater who lives in Lavenham now.

Went on again 4-6 very hot some body an S S Waller got up and broke one or two ribs for another, came off at 8, to get ready for a church, in the camp after we were dismissed so we went to see Lucy and back in camp half past eleven, after a very interesting evening was down for a (HBG) harbour boat guard.

25.1. Went on parade and a bath in afternoon, we had to get ready for 48 hour on the P.O.W. They started leave for the gerries. I rose at half past nine on the main gate, check on passes, it was a grand day and some more came in for the cellars.

On the 4-6 supper at half seven then 10-12 again. I was taken off guard to take Lt Vance to Rendsburg to get some shoes in the jeep at night, late back for my date. Another job on POW escort to watch on gerries loading coal. Went up the Bellevue to have a cuppa, the afternoon I found time for fretting, Saturday was a real lousy day went on parade at 8, then to a new billet had a sleep all afternoon and got in at 3am from Lucy.

Sunday get ready for church parade in the barracks on the Keil Harbour front, after that free for the rest of the day. Monday the watchmaker was allowed out of the wik camp on a pass, providing he came in at night and had his pass stamped. But he didn't return Monday night. I was on guard 48 hours at the time, about 9am his pal came to the gate and asked for pals kit. He was allowed in but a half track and 15 cwt were laid on to go and get him, by taking his pal with us. We told his pal not to speak to him but to put his kit in a door way and walk away. We backed the vehicles in yards, when we saw our man come along, I was to close in behind him, with a sten gun, my pal Harry came to his side with a rifle we marched him to the half track and said get in.

His next session was not too good, he was handed over to the German high up punishment court marshal, a big wheel barrow loaded with 155 mm shells. He had to trot round their vast parade ground six times every morning, he lasted for just three mornings and fell in the barrow that was his lot dead.

I continued after on guard, our little capture. I went on mobile patrol round the dock area it rained really hard had diner and cleaned up for another 48 hours. This was wik camp still got about 800 in there.

Monday 23rd July. We packed up kit to move again to fresh barracks called Essex we all had steel locker and key for kit, and bunk beds, very good place looked like their navy place. In the dining room a German painter had come in and painted the core signs of the second army they were very good.

Got time to get settled in then for another 48 hour guard. This one was a strange guard to us all the entrance was covered in rubber rings on the ground, some navy men were working on the U boat there, he looked and laughed and said that was the condom store for the German navy, they like plenty, so Pete and I had a look round first, but we chose the 2-4 shift, the place had window panes about 4' square with a lead surround, so we looked through and saw several boxes of bottles, as the coast was clear.

In the grass we saw a piece of steel tube we needed a piece of string yes, all tools complete we took out one pane of glass, wound the string round the end and put a slip loop in. then slid the tube in to lasso the bottle and wind up, hey presto a bottle of sherry. Hid it.

The laugh came in the morning when an officer came down and in, had a look round and missed a bottle from a full case of sherry. He told the guard commander he would check our kit before we left, bad luck chum it was taken care off.

Got up about 6am and wash ready to go at 10am when they took a lot of Hitler youth from the ship and deloused them, ready for wik camp. I lay on my old bed after a visit to the dentist to have a tooth plugged.

On the 26th I was on another 48 hour on the officers wine store, we didn't think we would get another one. This time we watched the German soldiers and their loved ones through stethoscopes very interesting. The spotter plane was up to keep an eye on them for the afternoon, they came from wik p.o.w camp by boat on the Keil canal.

Tuesday 21st. I went on sick parade as we were down for marching drill under Captain Taylor (Bluey), so I got off that and the day after a trip was going round the harbour a grand day. Sun was hot had a stroll up the Bellevue with Jack Everett, well we got a start into another month now.

July 3rd. a lovely day I went on a detail to Lubeck took our 15 cwt there was many spitfires buzzing went out with Jack White, Albert and Harry on guard house. I am another year older and good weather we are getting. Some of the troop moving to Remsburg to another camp, some of us spare bodies went there to clear up, it had been used by German waaf who left it in terrible state, glad to get back to Kiel took some lads to Rensberg and this will be a new sort of centre to treat the lads with 48 hours of penicillin every 2 hours. Later on they did a good trade.

Wednesday 15th. VJ day. We were given 2 days off and heard of 21 army had a big firework display stayed to watch it I looked at the board to see what guard I was on, went on 8-10 Hbu. Was easy one the weather changed to rain hard, went on to mobile column much better than walking round, I saw Gorings car big Mercedes stood on the quayside with more no telling where they went.

Saturday 24th. Came off patrol and the rest of the day free to get kit packed up next morning up at half five and start for Hamburg by lorry to a camp ankle deep in mud. We left at 4pm and got to Amsterdam at 10pm then went for a meal, had 3 hours break and were put on the train to the hook of Holland and sailed out at 9pm, busy day arrived in

Harwick at 6am and unloaded caught the 8.20 to Bury arrived 9.25 a lot of travelling for 10 days leave.

Had venture to Clacton for the day, next day father and mother persuaded me to go with them by train I had 20 minute walk to the hotel for breakfast had a look at the Mulberry exhibition, it was hot all day on the Saturday in the park listened to a band which pop great pleasure not if had to march with it.

August 3rd. Visit the market and had to take a blinking bone shaking old tram along to Portobello half hour walk and back to lunch. This was long enough for me, so at 10.40 I caught the coach to Motherwell where I was stationed once that lasted six months learning to drive tracked s.p guns 105mm, also invasion schemes I went to see the Brogan family who were good to us lads, I couldn't leave Cathie the girlfriend out, spent the rest of the day there. Caught the London train got in 10.30. Had a wash and brush up got rid of the scotch dust, made way round to see another old friend Katie Brown, spent the rest of the day with her.

Friday 7th. Was a nice day met Southey at Cambridge had a walk by the river cam and pictures. Back to Risby to get my kit together and ready to be on my way back, I made time to give R Bobys a look before going to Harwich 15.30. Woke up at 5.30 and had breakfast back on the train again at 10.30 bound for Nijmagen and on to Minden. Stop here for bacon sandwich and drink of tea, off to sleep until next that was Hamburg Altomia. Here I got off and went to 7RHU, left here at 11.30 by truck for Kiel and farmillio site. In the evening went with Jack to remember to fetch some lads back who had found some frau's of easy virtue and paid the price.

Wednesday 12th. Back to the grinder L.A.D guard came of at 11 and went for dinner it was a roast for a change, cooked by gerries, our tea was no match for dinner, had rest on my bed then to the Bellevue came back clean for top brass for the next guard and this about we get now. LGG on the front harbour no sooner come off this guard and look at the list to see the lot for 24 hour RG.

August 23rd. Went on mobile patrol some street in Kiel which gave us the chance to make friends with a few more frauleins like Helqu and Hette, I think they wanted to give Taffy and I a break by taking us to a holiday camp at Sehanlrest for 5 days. Had a walk round the place before dark. Hot water was brought round for washing and breakfast at 8am. It was a glorious day. So we went to the beach not far to walk at Timmedorfe-stranda, lashings of legless Germans here, hospitals were full. August 25 stayed on the beach all morning with a rather cheeky girl and the afternoon in the noon plenty of ATS here, but frauleins were much preferred. Well our time is up here but has made a nice break and had lovely weather. Had a good lunch and left at 1.30pm got to Kiel at 3.30. Went up Bellevue not much doing so I had an early night. Got ready to go on a 48hour at wik camp at 10. Cold and wet had a check up on the POW's in the noon I was changed over to patrol from the main gate. Then on search of missing kit. Following this lot of gerries another 300 came in for search and go to be deloused.

September 8th. Was time we went down town to see what's doing, Harry and I had a walk because many of the folk lived in their cellars since that's the best they had. One place had just a curtain blowing across where a door was missing, so Harry looked in to see a table and a military police cap and belt and pistol, this cap went walkies, the red cloth was removed, as we went on to find a gate post to stretch it over, while he enjoyed himself in another room. We looked for a tree to hang the cap. Right for goose, some foe gander.

Tuesday 9th. Back on 48 hour guard down the officers wine store again, mustn't nick any more this time, as they had moved a box away from the window. We heard a soldier had been caught from Hanover charged with desertion and robbery, for stealing a car and violence that was a court marshal for him.

After a long time since the gerry came down the hill fast in a town and hit the back of the 3 tonner I was driving, so about Wednesday 10th, I had to go on a charge before the Co as there was no damage to the lorry case was admonished. At 10, we went to a show at wik camp left of line on frating, and a film on VD, in the evening I went to the Empire and saw my frau, come on to rain hard just as well really. Those people love to get a good price some paid in other ways. Pete and I made good friends with a family by selling our ration of cigarettes and chocolates which we gave to their children. Marlot and Hajo, I used to correspond with them regular after I was demobbed, but I lost their address when they moved from Bremahaven, when they lived in Kiel we used to go to see them when we were not on a guard, Pete found a heap of coal in the trees behind the barracks this gradually disappeared for which they were grateful.

Sunday 21st. Mounted another 24 hour Regimental guard and a church parade for those not on guard or boat unit, some still out looking for an escaped soldier, I came off at 10am, rained hard all morning. Went up Bellevue. The dinner was fish the third successive meal not a very good advert. I slept as we were confined to barracks for an identity parade, last of the fish for supper.

Tuesday 23rd. On another 24 RG guard lousy day slipped up to Bellevue in the morning between shifts and strange to meet Anne on the way back, on at 11.30 and off at 12pm to 10am next morning, dismount and up on the bed until dinner, then in the afternoon went up to see Frieda's into bed about 11pm.

I don't get much free time now as so many lads have left for demob no sooner off one, than a 48 hour crop up, this one wik camp POW's it poured with rain made it uncomfortable for standing about, and a chat with frauleins asking for cigarettes or chocolate. We were given time to go to the canteen for a meal. Dismounted at 4.30 and above all the people watching was the Colonel, went for a bath, I then had tea and spent a pleasant evening at Frieda's, back to barracks round 11.50.

September 23rd. Just a few more guards and a job to take the half track into workshop for a new track and sprocket, it came up really foggy 19-20 groups were getting ready for return to the UK for demob. They had bad luck the lorry had a crash near Neamunter, sent another truck to take them on.

Up at 7.30 for a change I went to workshops to collect the half track, then on to odour camp and got 455 men to take them to Newsomme their future camp, our run back the roads were bad. We stayed in Hamburg where we got a puncture which was unusual we spent the night in Hamburg no hurry back, only to get another guard.

On Wednesday 7th had a football match between E troop and F at the wik camp. Took a truck to Rensburg for stores and brought back 4 lads it poured with rain the whole day, we had a room inspection if ok we were free to please ourselves, day off.

Sunday 11th November. I went to church parade on my return I had a telegram from home saying father had died in the WSGH from heart, so they told me to pack up what I wanted to take. Monday I went to brigade HQ and got a pass for 11 days, by plane Lt Braine drove me to Slegwik-Holstein up on the Danish border. Where an ATS girl and myself had a Stirling bomber, no seats and rattled like a lot of tin cans. We left at 1pm and arrived in Chelmsford at 2pm and home at 6.30pm.

Tuesday 13th. Went up to what 11.30 and his funeral at 2.30. Went to Bury in the morning next day I went to the west lines and saw the adjutant who asked if I would like compassionate posting. He said they could get my papers transferred. I said I would go back as I hadn't long to go. But it took much longer to get back. I left Bury on the 4th December got to Hanover late then to Hamburg at 8 after 28 hours of travel. I got to Neumunster at 4am had something to eat before starting to hitch a lift to Kiel. Many of the old boys had left for demob.

December 12th. Up at 5.25am for some sort of a scheme it was very cold and the roads very slippery. In the afternoon went on a demolition party at the Aoral house, the blast killed a sea full, at 1830 I took a leave party to the station and a ride round and took the fraulein home.

Thursday 5th. Was a day of high wind and rain took the truck to Rensburg and returned about seven. The short leave folk got back from Amsterdam. In the evening I got right under the blanket at 8.30. Force gale blowing.

Wednesday 19th. Captain Bluatt returned from leave and 9am parade and afterwards did a bit to the MH draining one tank and got ¾ of a gallon of water. In the afternoon I went to see the mo for my demob medical. A.1.

I wrote three letters then in the evening Jack and I went to the navy canteen for a meal, ours was chronic, then saw one of the Frauleins home, and had an early night.

December 20th. Next day I moved the half-track to its new place and blocked it up, took out the battery, later Jack and I went out to increase our marks!! That was quite a good night I made 180 marks. Went for a cuppa at the navy before turning in.

Saturday 22nd. The unit put on a party for the little ones at naval canteen and went on until 9.30. Went to the

Bellevue for a cuppa when four MP's came in, we thought they might have been looking for a spare hat, bad luck chum, saw Frieda on the way back had a late night, not so many guards now so many lads have gone home.

Sunday 23rd. went on parade at the garrison church several were there, laid on the bed until 12ish, I stayed in for the afternoon to write a few letters. In the evening Jack and I walked to the empire, some ATS have just arrived to cook for Sergeants mess. Next day I spent at the LAD took the Bren gun carrier out on test, and took a tilt to cover the half-track. Some of the lads had a bit of a party and got really oiled up.

Tuesday 25th. Another xmas day has come round up at 8.30, breakfast consisted of egg and bacon and sausage, went to rest on my bed until dinner at 1300, turkey, pork, sprouts, roast spuds, apple sauce. And an issue of 50 cigarettes, beer, plum pudding and custard. For tea we had jam cake and jellies and mince pies. Went for a walk and had a game with two frau's near our billet, they were happy old girls into my bed 11.30pm.

December 27th. In the morning I went on parade for a change it was not such a good day, came on to rain hard we had on the naval and the afternoon we had to go on a lecture by some old professor from Cambridge, I met two really old pals there Geoff Bowen and George, in the evening Jack and I had a walk out to see how many old scratches were out.

Friday 28th. Signed to take over a 3 tonner for general carrying of stores etc. took on for more lads of 20 group to the station to start their home ward trip for demob. Captain Bluey being one, good to see him go. For tea I had a bit of fish after which I went up to Frieda and the last of the 24's leave this day, not so long now before the 25 group pack off. Another guard came into being and it came on to snow very hard.

January 3rd 1946. It was a cold day got caught for regimental guard this maybe my last. I went on 1st shift there weren't many people out, my next shift 10-12 then on the bed warmer inside.

One more 24 hour came off at 6pm some big brass man came to look so we had to give the room a sweep through.

January 5th. Got up early they wanted the half track got ready to go and more petrol from the dump at scheleing got in late. I think the food situation has gone downhill just to get such a small piece of fish in butter was a job to feel it in ones mouth.

Thursday 10th. Very cold out, moved the half-track to a yard at the scheleing. Went up to Mordmark for most the morning. I did all my webbing with new Blanco in the evening my boots got their boning to standard.

Friday 11th. I had to rise a bit earlier to mount yet another guard. It was a terrific day rain and gale force wind which prevented the boots going out. This day 1946 the family moved from Risby to Bury.

The 3 tonner was late coming for us, arriving at 11pm, had an early night after that. On Saturday up about 8am and had a very small piece of spam, I nearly choked on it. In the morning the CO had an inspection of the room. If it didn't come up to scratch no Bellevue. Marvellous what a bucket of water would do, he came back but the room was empty, all gone that's the second time.

Tuesday 15th. At the hour of 6 I was on the go with the truck roads in a bad state of frozen ice and snow, several thrills to keep it on the road to Hamsburg got to Kiel at 9.30 worth a swig of rum, it was freezing ride. No heater on army trucks so went up to Frieda's house 20-12 late.

Thursday 17th. I was on my last RG for George and his country, and it was freezing hard to make it a bitter wind got up, came off at 12pm to have a hot cuppa, next morning still cold. They caught up on Upton one of them I bet he thought he was clear, went up to the Bellevue with Joe Hubbard at 3pm. Went up the navy canteen to see if anything was afoot only a fight between drunkies. I left and went to 117 for the evening, left there at 12.40 my bed was calling very frosty and moonlight.

Sunday 20th. Laid in bed until 9.15 then down on pay parade to pick up the marks, and to the navy better food than our cooks turn out, did a bit off packing the old junk in the old kit bag. Went to the Empire with George Formby, wrote an odd letter saying the last of Kiel.

Monday 21st. so this is my last day here, all kit packed up and handed in, went to say cheerio to Marlot and Hajo old friends ready for the off.

Tuesday 22nd. Got up at 0500 and had a good breakfast and left at 7.30am , the train was late so we left at Retenburg until 17.30, only to return to Hamsburg Altonia by truck to start again, very cold going all day and night at 4.30.

Wednesday 23rd. still going but not so fast, had a good meal at Minden and a kip the train was quite warm for a change early morning, got to Tournai. Had a bit of sleep, up at 7.30 for breakfast.

Thursday 24th. Here all day scheming how to change all my marks, changed into Francs for a start, thousands of them. Laid on the bed most of the morning next to my old mate Pete, also thinking how to get round it, part was to go round twice to a different man paying out, the rest I leave unwritten but it worked and we managed it ok, two heads better than one. In the afternoon another job to all my francs changed to sterling, what a big fiddle but in the end it worked. Had tea and early night to bed, my conscience kept me awake.

Friday 25th. Got up at 5.30 and had a little to eat and ready to move on, next stop 7.30am. Got on the train heading for Calais and it was a nice day, met Frank Apps (trapper), also going home for demob 25 group. We went into the camp for food, left here at 14.20 very rough for our trip to Dover, the engine broke down, so we got to Reading at 01.30, and stayed the night or what was left of it.

Saturday 24th. Up at 0700 about to give our kit in at 10pm, left here for the last stage at Northampton.

Sunday 27th. At 1900 got a train for Cambridge at 0130 waited here until 0820 for the slow train to Bury St Edmunds, and home Saturday and talked, bed at 2300 hours.

18.7.39 - 27.1.46